Derbyshire, Nottinghamshire and Lincolnshire

CHARLES WILDGOOSE
AND ROGER FOX

COUNTRYSIDE BOOKS
NEWBURY BERKSHIRE

First published 2005
© Charles Wildgoose, 2005
© Roger Fox, 2005

COUNTRYSIDE BOOKS
3 Catherine Road
Newbury, Berkshire

To view our complete range of books,
please visit us at
www.countrysidebooks.co.uk

ISBN 1 85306 900 0

Photographs by the authors

Produced through MRM Associates Ltd., Reading
Typeset by Mac Style Ltd, Scarborough, N. Yorkshire
Printed by Woolnough Bookbinding Ltd., Irthlingborough

Contents

INTRODUCTION

WALKS IN DERBYSHIRE

WALKS IN NOTTINGHAMSHIRE

Contents

WALKS IN LINCOLNSHIRE

PUBLISHER'S NOTE

We hope that you obtain considerable enjoyment from this book; great care has been taken in its preparation. However, changes of landlord and actual closures are sadly not uncommon. Likewise, although at the time of publication all routes followed public rights of way or permitted paths, diversion orders can be made and permissions withdrawn.

We cannot, of course, be held responsible for such diversion orders and any inaccuracies in the text which result from these or any other changes to the routes nor any damage which might result from walkers trespassing on private property. We are anxious though that all details covering the walks are kept up to date and would therefore welcome information from readers which would be relevant to future editions.

However, for the benefit of a proper map, we do recommend that you purchase the relevant Ordnance Survey sheet covering your walk. The Ordnance Survey maps are widely available, especially through booksellers and local newsagents.

Introduction

The countryside around Tideswell

In Derbyshire, Nottinghamshire and Lincolnshire, you have three very different counties. Derbyshire, with its high peaks and far-reaching views, is a walker's paradise, whilst Nottinghamshire, with its canals and woods, offers the chance to tread gently and marvel at the wild-life. Lincolnshire, with its wide skies and network of paths, ancient and modern, is the ideal county for getting far away from the madding crowds.

The routes chosen in Derbyshire give you the opportunity to sample some of the best of the Peak District when setting out from Tideswell; the chance to marvel at the engineering feat that is the Ladybower Reservoir; and walk along some of the county's many long-distance paths, including the Tissington Trail and the High Peak Trail. In Nottinghamshire, you can walk through Sherwood Forest and visit the Major Oak, stroll the county's many canals including the Chesterfield and Grantham canals; visit historic villages such as Laxton and take to the paths through majestic Clumber Park. In Lincolnshire, you can enjoy a fenland walk from Surfleet, discover little visited hamlets near Sleaford and marvel at the splendid scenery in the Wolds when setting out from Belchford.

The range of pubs is just as diverse as the routes themselves: from inns steeped in history through to modern, airy, hostelries but they all have one thing in common – a warm welcome. Do remember, though, that if you intend to leave your car in the pub car park whilst on the walk, it is only polite to mention it to the landlord beforehand. and, when you return, make sure you leave any muddy boots at the door before entering the pub for that well-earned drink.

The sketch maps that accompany the walks are intended to give you an overall view of the route to be followed but for more detailed information we do advise you to carry the relevant OS maps, too. It is also a good idea to pack a drink and some waterproofs.

Enjoy the walks – we are sure you will. There's some cracking scenery and some excellent pubs, so pull on those boots!

Charles Wildgoose and Roger Fox

LOCATION OF THE WALKS

Nottinghamshir

N

Buxton
Bakewell

Chesterfield

Worksop

Matlock

Ashbourne

Mans
South

Derby

Nottingh

Derbyshire

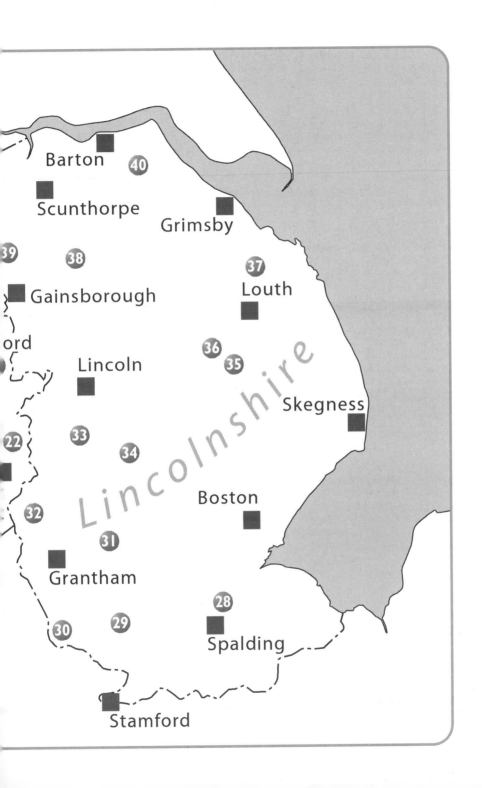

Barton
Scunthorpe
Grimsby
40
39
38
Louth
37
Gainsborough
ord
Lincoln
36
35
Skegness
33
22
34
Boston
32
31
Grantham
28
30
29
Spalding
Stamford

Lincolnshire

Ladybower Reservoir
The Famous Yorkshire Bridge Inn

One of the longer walks with excellent views. It's good to see Bamford Mill has been preserved by being converted to private apartments and the old chapel in Thornhill which is now a private home (with gravestones in the garden). The homeward stretch involves a climb up the lower slopes of Win Hill but stunning views of Ladybower make it all worthwhile.

The **Famous Yorkshire Bridge Inn** is a friendly, efficient and welcoming pub. Make sure you drop in after your walk. You won't be disappointed. There's an excellent choice of food. You're spoilt for choice. Why not try Cajun chicken with Louisianna sauce or a pair of lamb steaks 'sizzler'. Two of my favourite beers here too – Timothy Taylor Landlord and Theakstons Old Peculier.

Opening times are 11 am to 11 pm (food available 12 noon to 2 pm and 6 pm to 9 pm, though on a Sunday from 12 noon to 8.30 pm).

Telephone: 01422 651361.

Distance: 7¼ *miles*

OS OL1 The Dark Peak
GR 202860

A challenging walk. If there's been heavy rain, it may not be possible to cross the river at Bamford Mill. If so continue along the disused railway line [see [3] below] to reach the 'square-ish house built by the Derwent Valley Water Board'.

Starting point: Heatherdene car park, half a mile north of the pub.

How to get there: The Famous Yorkshire Bridge Inn is on the A6013 north of Bamford.

The Walk

1 Heatherdene car park marks the start of the Derwent Valley Heritage Way. Look out for the yellow and purple waymarks. Walk to the southern end of the car park passing the toilets. Follow the signs for Ladybower Dam. Away to the right above the dam is Win Hill. Ladybower when full holds 6.1 billion gallons of water. It opened on the 25th September 1945. A few hundred yards from the car park, descend the steps to the road. This brings you to the memorial commemorating the opening of the dam.

2 Cross the road as though you're going to cross the dam wall. Instead, take the footpath on the nearside by the large metal gates. Descend into the valley (signed 'Win Hill'). Ignore a path to the left. Turn left though on reaching a track. Stay on this to reach a road. Turn right across the Derwent. Bear left beyond. Some 40 yards later, bear right along the path rising through the brambles (for

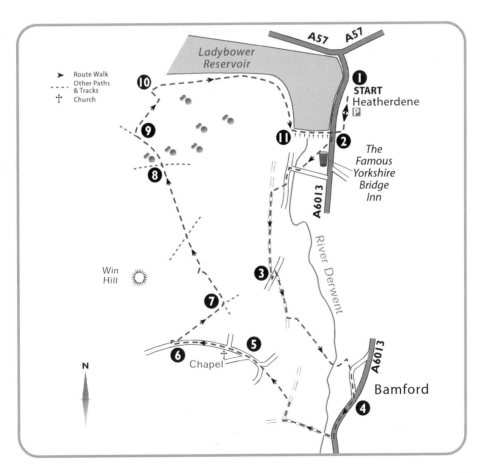

Bamford Edge

Thornhill). This brings you to a disused railway line. Turn left.

❸ Half a mile later you reach a lane. Cross this and follow the Derwent Valley Heritage Way beyond, still along the old railway line. Cross a private driveway. In 100 yards, turn left and cross a stile. Descend to a track and turn right. Pass through a gateway, then pass a stone barn. Shortly after, pass through another gateway before keeping in the same direction to a gateway 100 yards ahead. Walk towards Bamford Mill in the long field beyond. Cross the footbridge over the Derwent to reach the mill. Keep forward to reach a drive. Turn right, then 50 yards later, right again at 1 Peartree Cottage, keeping the mill on your right as you go. Continue down the access lane to the main road.

❹ Turn right for 250 yards before turning sharp right along Water Lane. Cross the river again. Continue past the recreation ground on the left. Eventually you reach a square-ish house built by Derwent Valley Water Board. Turn right on the path immediately beyond this property. This takes you across the Derwent Valley Heritage Way. Head up the path beyond, initially with a sunken lane down to your left. In 400 yards you reach the lane in Thornhill. Turn right uphill, then first left along the lane.

❺ When the lane forks 100 yards later, ignore the left fork, continue past the old chapel on your left, with graves in its garden. On reaching Town Head Lane to the right, pass through the gap in the wall on your left. Turn right walking through the fields for $^1/_2$ mile with the lane on your right.

6 Ignore an opening onto the lane as you go, but on reaching a stile immediately before two gates set at right angles to each other, cross it and turn right along the lane, heading back the way you've come. Less than 100 yards later cross a squeezer stile on the left. With your back to this head half right across the field. Keep in the same direction, perhaps slightly left, in the second field and the subsequent ones to reach the top end of a wood rising from the right. Walk past the pumping station to reach the cross-paths.

7 Turn left uphill for Win Hill. Stay beside the wall/fence on your left. A marvellous view of Ladybower opens out. Pass through a farmgate and continue as before. Then go through a wicket gate. Keep beside the wall on your left for 50 yards before turning sharp right up the grassy path. Stay on this path, rising steadily uphill. On reaching a wall, bear right for Win Hill, keeping the wall on your left. This is a fairly level path. Where it forks 400 yards later, stay on the lower one beside the wall.

8 On entering the trees, keep forward at the cross-paths. In 300 yards pass through a gate and, with Winhill Pike uphill to your left, bear right downhill. After 50 yards bear slightly left through the heather to a gate 200 yards away.

9 Turn sharp right through this. Proceed through the trees to a stile. Beyond there's a marvellous view of Crook Hill. Follow the path that descends ahead of you. It then bears right downhill after 300 yards. In 200 yards turn left along a level track that takes you down to the main track around the dam. If you go astray just keep descending to this track.

10 Turn right. A mile later you reach the dam wall.

11 Cross this to return to your car.

Date walk completed:

....

Place of Interest Nearby
Peveril Castle at Castleton, built by William the Conqueror's son, and now in the care of English Heritage, is well worth a visit. And why not visit the caverns whilst you're there. Call Castleton Tourist Information Centre on 01433 670207.

Bretton, near Foolow
The Barrel Inn

An excellent Peak District walk in an area beloved by peakland aficionados. It may be a bit taxing as you return from the delights around Stoke Ford but it will be well worth it – and the views from Bretton are not to be sniffed at.

The **Barrel Inn**, built at the end of the 16th century, is a pub with character. It is a real walker's pub, one that you will like as soon as you walk in through the front door. The food is super, too, with dishes out of the ordinary usually available, like Cooperman's Pie. If you want something a bit more run of the mill then there are omelettes, jacket potatoes, hot Ciabatta rolls and cheese and leek crumble.

Opening times are 9 am to 3 pm and 6 pm to 11 pm weekdays. Saturdays 11 am to 11pm and Sundays 12 noon to 10.30 pm. Food is available every day from 12 noon to 2.30 pm and 6.30 pm to 9.30 pm (Sunday to 9 pm).

Telephone: 01433 630856.

Distance: *4½ miles*

OS OL24 The White Peak
GR 201779

A short walk but it can prove a little testing.

Starting point: The field at the side of the Barrel Inn. Park at the pub or the roadside above. Please do not park in front of the pub.

How to get there: Foolow is a couple of miles east of Tideswell. From Foolow head due north along a minor road. Stay on this road to reach the Barrel at the top of the hill.

The Walk

❶ With your back to the Barrel, turn left along the road. In 500 yards fork left along the grassy track between walls. Nearly 300 yards later, turn right on joining another track. This brings you back to the road you were on earlier!

❷ Turn left along the tarmac lane. After 50 yards, as the road swings sharp right, keep forward along the rougher track ahead. This is Sir William Hill Road and runs in a straight line for 1³/₄ miles. You only stay on it for just under 1 mile until it reaches another road coming in from the right.

❸ Here you should turn sharp left on the first of two paths whose stiles are close together on your left. The one you want has a Peak & Northern Footpath sign (No. 78) at the beginning. Walk alongside the wall on your right through the heather. Stay on the obvious path beside the wall

for ³/₄ mile until it swings left away from the wall. Good views of Hathersage appear on your right as you proceed. The wall rejoins the path. On reaching a grassy path running uphill to your left alongside another wall, turn right towards two gates 30 yards away. Cross the step-over to the left of the left-hand gate.

❹ Proceed along the grassy track ahead with a wall on your right and a steep slope on your left. You will see a ruin below – you will be walking past this before too long and heading up the fields directly away from where you are. The track you're on swings right. Cross another step-over by a gate. The track then swings left and descends further into the clough, and a number of oak trees. A stream is now down to your right. On reaching a path dropping downhill from left to right, turn left uphill. (If you descend down this to your right you reach Stoke Ford – an attractive spot where a number of paths meet.)

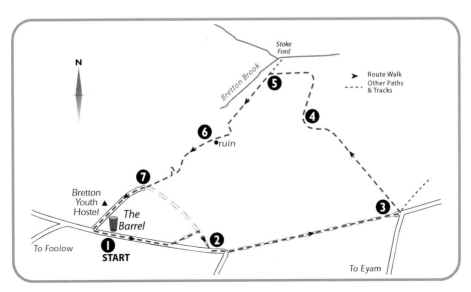

A marvellous view along the way

5 So, you rise uphill steadily. Bretton Brook is down to your right. Cross a step-over as you proceed. Some 500 yards after joining this path it runs alongside a fence on your right before swinging right over a stream. Rise up the steep grassy bank with the ruin you saw earlier on your left. Though steep this stretch of path is soon over!

6 Keep straight ahead through the fields beyond the ruin. Pass through a number of tumble-down walls on a fairly level path. The path then narrows from a wide grassy one and you find yourself walking around a bank stretching uphill to your left. This takes you into ferns and hawthorns though shortly you're back out in the open. You should be rising gently with steeper ground on your left. Then you bear left beside a fence on your right before crossing a stile to then swing right uphill. In 30 yards bear left uphill, subsequently swinging right, to a seat in memory of a lady called Winifred Woods. Turn left uphill here. Follow the fenced path to walk past a property on your left to reach a narrow tarmac lane.

7 Turn right. This takes you all the way back to the Barrel.

Date walk completed:

....

Place of Interest Nearby

The village of **Eyam** which suffered so much during the Great Plague is worth exploring. There are plaques in the village explaining where the plague started. Visit Eyam Museum, telephone 01433 631371, and Eyam Hall, telephone 01433 631976, though the Hall isn't open all year round.

The George Hotel

Archetypal Peak District scenery is the order of the day if you follow this walk. There's an added bonus because you'll be able to use a 'new' footpath which runs along the western edge of Litton Frith, a lovely wood rising up above Cressbrookdale.

Distance: 5¼ miles

OS OL Map 24 The White Peak
GR 154742

A bit of an 'up-and-downer' but fine if you take it steady.

Starting point: Tideswell Dale car park.

How to get there: Turn south-westwards off the A623 for Tideswell. Pass the George on the right and continue down the road for 1 mile to reach the Tideswell Dale car park on the left.

The George stands next to the Cathedral of the Peak, the magnificent church of St John the Baptist. An old coaching house, it is a popular pub, usually particularly busy on a Sunday, and welcomes everyone. It is renowned for its food and rightly so. With bar meals offering steak and kidney ale pie and battered haddock and main courses, including prime local gammon steak and seafood such as home-made seafood crumble, you will see there's a wide range of dishes. Hardys and Hansons beer is the order of the day if you want a drink.

Opening times Weekdays 12 noon to 3 pm and 6 pm to 11 pm. Weekends, particularly in summer, it tends to be open all day from 12 noon onwards

Telephone: 01298 871382

The Walk

1 Walk towards the car park entrance taking the path to the right of it signed 'Tideswell Village'. Walk beneath a line of beech trees parallel to the road on your left. On reaching the road follow the concessionary path in the field with the road still on your left.

2 Turn right at the road junction for Litton. In 500 yards, just before the first house on the right in Litton, take the path on your right up the right side of the field

and in the top right corner, cross the lane. Follow the obvious path in the first two fields proceeding along the left side of the next three fields to reach a lane.

3 Continue along the lane. Keep forward on the track, where it bends left. Ten yards later, turn right over the stile and walk down the first field. Bear left across the corner of the second field, in the general direction of Wardlow Hay Cop, the hill with the trig point on top. Bear *slightly* right in the next field, aiming between the top left corner and

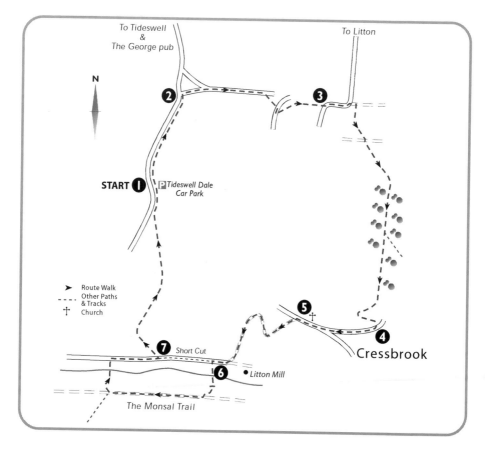

Going down towards Litton Mill

the gate. Cross the track and keep in the same general direction as before through the next two fields, aiming for the top left corner of the following field. Cut the corner of the next field and, when you reach the woodland of Litton Frith, turn right to walk along the top side of the wood. This, at present, is a bit of a challenge. Some 400 yards later the path descends quite steeply down a flight of steps. Do not descend them but fork right taking the path that keeps on the top side of the wood. This isn't as well used as the other one so you need to take care as there is a drop to your left as you go. Stay on this for 350 yards. Leave the woodland and proceed straight through the long field, with trees to your left, for 350 yards. At the far end of the field pass through a wicket gate and bear right

towards some houses. On reaching the first house, turn left and walk down the side of it turning left just a few yards later to walk down a walled path to the lane.

❹ Turn right and walk through Cressbrook village. Between the houses on the left you'll get a glimpse of their marvellous view. Keep forward ignoring a sharp left turn to reach the church of St John the Evangelist.

❺ In 75 yards bear left along a track signed 'Litton Mill' and 'Millers Dale'. Once you're out of the trees a superb view of Millers Dale opens out with High Field above. You may see on the opposite side of the valley someone walking the Platelayers Path, even though it isn't a public footpath. Many people walk it and in fact it now crosses access land. Pass through a gate, continuing down the grassy track beyond. Cross a stile by another gate bearing left beyond towards a chimney. Follow the grassy track as it swings downhill to the right and then to the left to take you down to the recently renovated Litton Mill.

6 At the gateposts (Litton Mills) turn right. (*you can stay on the road for 350 yards to reach point [7] or read on!*) Turn left beyond a building, signed Monsal Trail, passing to the left of Litton Mill Sewage Pumping Station. Cross the bridge and zigzag up to the Monsal Trail. Turn right along this for nearly 1/2 mile. Where a path rises uphill on your left into the nature reserve, turn right down the path for Ravenstor. Descend the steps

and cross the bridge to reach a road. Turn right here beside the Wye. In 600 yards turn sharp left up the path, just beyond a small parking area, for Tideswell Dale.

7 Follow the path up the dale. When it splits, take the right fork over the footbridge bearing left beyond it, ignoring a concession path up steps to the right. When the path you're on is joined by another from the left, keep on up the dale. Subsequently ignore the path turning sharp right to the picnic site. Keep on up the dale to the car park.

Date walk completed:

Place of Interest Nearby
Take the time to walk around the **Cathedral of the Peak** next door to the George Hotel. This is rightly regarded as one of the most impressive churches in the area. Built in the 14th century, it has altered little over the years and replaced an earlier Norman church.

The Kelstedge Inn

Straddling the boundary between the Derbyshire Dales and North East Derbyshire this walk takes you through the fields of Rushley Lodge Farm.

Distance: 6¼ miles

OS Explorer 269 Chesterfield and Alfreton and OL24 The White Peak GR 339638

Fairly firm underfoot with just a couple of climbs.

Starting point: The pub car park. Please ask the landlord's permission before leaving your car whilst you walk or park on the road nearby.

How to get there: Kelstedge is on the A632, some 3 miles north-east of Matlock.

The **Kelstedge Inn** used to be a blacksmith's and you can see the remains of the forge in the fireplace on your right as you walk in. This is a very homely walker-friendly pub so you've no excuse not to visit. Sandwiches and jacket potatoes are on offer, as well as more refined fare such as beef in red wine. There is an excellent beer selection, with Bass, Stones and Abbot Ale, completing the line-up.

Opening times are Monday to Thursday, 12 noon to 3 pm and 7 pm to 11 pm; Friday, Saturday and Sunday: 12 noon to 11 pm.

Telephone: 01246 590448.

Walk 4 *Kelstedge*

The Walk

1 From the Kelstedge Inn, cross the A632 and walk along Vernon Lane, opposite. After passing various properties, the views open out to your left. At the gateway of Amber House, keep forward on the bridleway into the trees. In the wood, the bridleway is easy to follow. Cross a simple bridge after 250 yards, ignoring a footpath on the right just beyond. Cross another bridge 200 yards later. Stay on the bridleway as it rises, winding through the countryside. Pass Vernon Lane Farm on your left. Beyond, at the gateway to this property, bear right along the driveway to a lane.

2 Turn left past Eddlestow Lot car park on the left. In 200 yards you reach a T-junction. Cross the road to the path opposite, entering Forest Enterprise land. There are two paths here. Take the left one and 300 yards later keep forward across a 'ride' in the wood. Some 400 yards after this, six paths meet. Taking the path you're on as number 1, count clockwise and follow number 4 – a straight path underneath pine trees. In 300 yards, bear right alongside the wall to Cuckoostone Lane ('Cuckerstn' to locals).

3 Turn right and in 550 yards reach a property. Keep forward along the track to

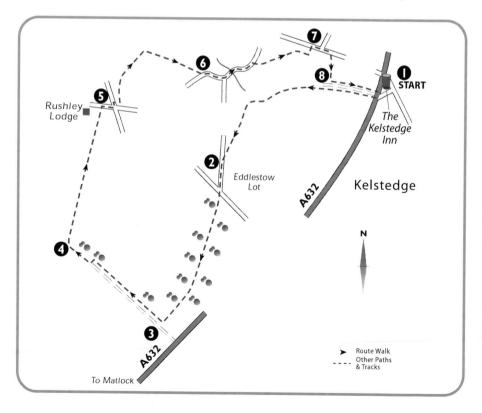

Route Walk
Other Paths & Tracks

20

A stone guide-post

the right of this. The golf course is to your left. Stay on the grassy track to enter a field. Keep forward on the right side of the fields with a wood on your right.

❹ At the corner of the wood bear right to the stile 30 yards away. These fields were reclaimed from moorland by Fred Wildgoose in the 1940s. Cross the large field heading diagonally across it. Aim 60 yards to the right of the far left corner. In the next field, keep in the same direction towards the long green-roofed 'barn' in the distance, passing through a squeezer stile, at present behind a muckheap! Rushley Lodge is ahead. Aim for the far right corner of the next field passing through the stile by the gate. Walk alongside the wall on your right for five yards before bearing half right towards

the gates in front of the barn. Pass through the right hand gate, walking across the field beyond to the gate opposite to reach Jaggers Lane.

❺ Turn right then left at the crossroads, past a guidepost in the wall. Some 30 yards later cross the wall on your right. The path should run half left but initially it heads directly away from the road, probably even slightly right, before bearing half left downhill. Keep just left of a single wooden electricity pole. Beyond this the path runs across a fairly flat area for 70 yards. Then you should bear slightly right into some trees and, in the corner of a 'field', pass through a gap. Bear right, walking between parallel walls beneath silver birches towards a property. Pass through a stile on your right near this property, then a second one beside a pond on your left. Keep the stream and the buildings to your left to reach and cross a small wooden bridge over a ditch, then a second one. Pass through a squeezer. At the driveway leading into the property on your left, bear right over a step-over by a gate. Follow the grassy track away from the property. In 600 yards you reach a lane.

6 Turn left and 400 yards later, at the T-junction beside Jaggers Cottage, turn left again, descending to Hodgelane Brook. The lane then rises steeply. Immediately beyond Whitefield House take the steps into the field. Walk alongside the wall on your right before bearing slightly left through the gaps in the boundaries of three fields to reach the far left corner of the third field. Cross the stile here and, keeping in the same direction, head towards the property ahead. Cross the

stile in front of an outbuilding. Turn right immediately to cross a stile beside a gate. Walk down the right side of the field beyond for 125 yards, passing through a stile in front of you. Keep forward for a few yards before turning left, between wall and hedge, to reach a lane.

7 Turn right. Ignore a road to the left after 100 yards but 150 yards later, after ignoring other paths, cross a stile by a gate on your right immediately before the stream. Walk along the well-defined path for 300 yards until it 'dives' into the trees. Pass through a gate to reach the bridleway used earlier.

8 Turn left back to Kelstedge.

Date walk completed:

Places of Interest Nearby
Visit **Matlock Bath** and enjoy a ride on the cable-car to the **Heights of Abraham** where you can stroll the woodland paths and admire the views or go underground to explore the caverns in the hillside. Telephone: 01629 582365.

The Elm Tree Inn

Heath is a lovely village and the surrounding countryside is an interesting area in which to walk. There is the opportunity to explore the ruins of Sutton Scarsdale Hall, the chance to wander through Sutton Springs Wood and the prospect of following the Five Pits Trail.

The **Elm Tree Inn** is worth seeking out. It's a friendly welcoming place, with good food and beer. It used to be a workhouse and there's a foreboding tunnel linking it with the old church nearby. Don't take the wrong door if you're going to the toilets! There are a couple of hand-pulled beers, usually Pedigree and a guest such as Adnams. The food is wide-ranging with old favourites such as scampi, cod and vegetable lasagne, together with something a bit different such as Chicken New York (chicken topped with bacon and cheese).

Opening times are Monday to Saturday 11.30 am to 3 pm and 5 pm til 11 pm; Sunday 12 noon to 3 pm and 6 pm to 10.30 pm.

Telephone: 01246 850490

Distance: 8¼ miles

OS Explorer 269 Chesterfield and Alfreton GR 447671

A longer walk but fairly easy, with no difficult climbs.

Starting point: The Elm Tree pub. Park in the vicinity of the church or at the pub, with the landlord's permission, of course.

How to get there: Take the Clay Cross road from Junction 29 of the M1. In ½ mile, turn right into Heath. The church and the pub are at the far end of the village.

23

The Walk

❶ Turn left from the pub along the road towards the church. On the right-hand bend, turn left down the track, for Palterton, Stockley Trail and Sutton Scarsdale. Stay on this, passing the churchyard on your right. Cross the bridge over the bypass. Immediately beyond turn left for Sutton Scarsdale. Walk parallel to the bypass to your left. In 200 yards, at the second of a pair of double electricity poles, turn right towards the left side of a wood across the valley. Descend into the valley, crossing a footbridge. Rise up the left side of the

hedge to reach the left side of the wood. Stay beside this to reach and cross a track. Keep forward to the far end of the wood. With the M1 approximately $1/2$ mile away, keep forward to the double gates ahead.

❷ On reaching another track turn left along it, rising towards a farm. Some 80 yards before it, turn right over a stile, proceeding down the right side of the field. Bear left in the wood in the valley. Cross a footbridge. Rise up under an electricity pylon. Then walk up the left side of the hedge leading away from you and 400 yards later reach a lane.

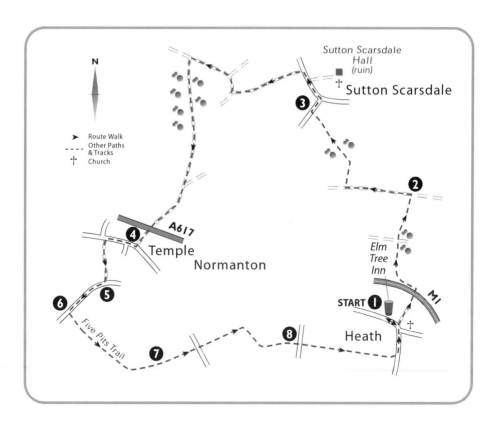

The ruins of Sutton Scarsdale Hall

❸ Turn right, swinging left into Sutton Scarsdale, ignoring the right turn to Palterton. In 200 yards a lane to the right leads to the remains of Sutton Scarsdale Hall and 100 yards beyond this lane turn left along Rock Lane. Ignore a footpath along a driveway to the left after 1/2 mile but 200 yards later swing right when the track forks. After 180 yards, fork left towards Sutton Springs Wood. In the trees, ignore a track on the right take the one to the left 20 yards later. Proceed through the woodland for 1/2 mile with various properties to your right. You're 3 miles from the centre of Chesterfield! Stay on the main track, ignoring a footpath to the left as you see the bypass a 1/4 mile ahead. Descend on the track, known as Postman's Lane, passing under the bypass.

❹ Ascend the road into Temple Normanton. Turn right at the main road. Stay on this for 600 yards descending the hill. Well before the traffic disappears round the sharp right-hand bend, get on the left side of the road, crossing with care, and follow the bridleway on the left, before the corner. Stay on this for 1/2 mile.

❺ At the lane turn right for 200 yards. Turn right into the car park of Grassmoor Country Park, then left along the path running parallel to the road you were following. This takes you to the Five Pits Trail.

❻ After 250 yards bear left under the roadbridge, following the trail. It rises uphill. It then bears left where, under some pylons, another gravel path joins from the right. Keep forward, bearing left here. After about 30 yards, the trail splits. Take the left fork for Williamthorpe.

7 You reach Wolfie Pond after 60 yards. Keep this on your right. Stay on the gravel path and ignoring forks to the left, pass under the road with the warehousing beyond. After 250 yards, on reaching a gravel path coming in from the left, bear right. Stay on the main gravel path ignoring all paths off it. You're soon walking beside a large modern warehouse/factory. One of the ponds, fed by minewater from Welbeck and Thoresby, Nottinghamshire, should be visible down to your right. Your gravel path swings left before descending into a valley. Ignore another gravel path to your left, to reach and cross a bridge over the stream taking water downhill to your

left. Ascend the steep path in front. At a crossroads of paths, keep forward for Holmewood. In 400 yards the path has levelled out. Turn left here along the grassy path for Heath and 100 yards later, with a field on your left, bear slightly right. This leads you along the back of some houses.

8 Cross a lane, taking the path opposite. Keep on the right side of three fields, walking towards Heath. Cross the stile in the middle of the bottom side, in the third field. Proceed to the main street. Turn left, following the road as it subsequently bends left, back to the pub.

Date walk completed:

....

Place of Interest Nearby
Hardwick Hall is signposted from Junction 29 of the M1. This National Trust property is a most impressive Elizabethan manor house and well worth a visit. Telephone: 01246 850430.

No lonesome trail for you today – we've got a pair of them – the High Peak Trail and the Tissington Trail. Two former railway lines that are now open to walkers, cyclists and, I believe, horse riders. The Tissington Trail was opened on the 5th June 1971. This walk links up a section of both trails and you also pass the brickworks at Friden where some excellent interpretation panels give you an insight into the working life of this industry.

Distance: *4½ miles*

OS OL24 The White Peak GR 149611

Gravel covered trails make up most of the route though there is some field walking. There is a bit of 'upping-and-downing' but nothing too taxing.

Starting point: Park at Hartington station on the Tissington Trail.

How to get there: From the A515 north of Newhaven, take the B5054 to the west for Hartington. Turn left at the sign for Hartington station on the Tissington Trail. To reach the Devonshire Arms turn left out of the car park to reach Hartington itself. The pub is on the left in the village.

The **Devonshire Arms** is a long, low pub in the middle of Hartington. It is much larger than you might imagine and very popular. With good beer, including Jennings' Cumberland and Greene King Abbot Ale plus a guest, and good food it's well worth driving down into Hartington to visit. There's plenty of choice too with dishes such as home-made chicken curry, fresh cod fillet, home-made lasagne verdi and wild mushroom lasagne. It's popular not just with walkers and visitors to the youth hostel up the road but locals, too.

Opening times are from 12 noon til 11 pm in summer, with food available from 12 noon to 3 pm and from 6 pm to 9.30 pm.

Telephone: 01298 84232.

The Walk

1 From the car park walk along the Tissington Trail away from the road. Pass an old disused quarry on the left. Then pass under a bridge, ignoring a footpath a few yards later on the left. Continue until you reach Ruby Wood on your left. There's a picnic site here and the chance to learn something about Muttley, a horse that used to be ridden on the trail by a local ranger. The trail starts to open out beyond the wood with Heathcote to your right and Biggin, half right. On a gradual right-hand bend, just beyond a couple of stone bridge foundations, climb the steps on your left to leave the trail.

2 In the first field, with your back to the stile, bear half right to pass through a stile. In the second field, head for another stile in the far top corner. At the next field walk past the pair of electricity poles and pass through a walled gap in the trees. Cross the step stile beside the gate. Walk through the long field ahead with Stanedge Grange to your right. Cross a substantial stone step-stile at the end of the field and two more directly beyond. Then cross another with the buildings at Newhaven ahead. Beyond this stile, skirt to the left of the buildings, keeping the buildings immediately to your right, to reach the road.

3 Cross the road carefully and keep left before, almost immediately, turning right

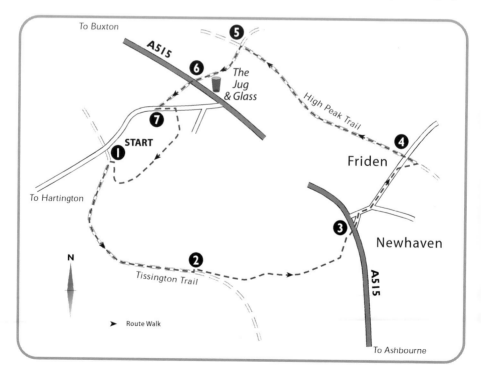

Hartington station on the Tissington Trail

you reach this main road, the Jug and Glass Inn is to your left.

6 Cross the A515 and walk along the track ahead. After a while this descends to a lane.

7 Turn left for 100 yards. Take the footpath on your right walking along the left side of the first and then second fields. The path descends to a wicket gate which you pass through. Descend the rough ground beyond for 60 yards or so crossing a stile to get into the field beyond. Walk across the field, aiming for the right-hand side of a line of trees ahead of you. Beyond the wicket gate walk straight forward along the path through the rough and slightly overgrown ground. This path should bring you to a step-over stile. Beyond this descend to the Tissington Trail and turn right back to your car.

on the road for Cromford and Matlock. After 100 yards, bear right again though it may be best to get on the other side of the road before the bend. Turn left along the road for Friden and 500 yards later fork right onto the High Peak Trail.

4 On reaching the High Peak Trail itself, turn left crossing the road that you recently left behind. Keep on the trail for another mile, crossing the drive to Brundcliffe Farm, immediately to the right of the trail, as you go.

5 On reaching a crossroads with Green Lane, turn left towards the A515. When

Date walk completed:

....

Place of Interest Nearby

After your pub stop, why not look around **Hartington**. The interesting shops include an excellent cheese shop by the duckpond.

Carsington Water
The Knockerdown

A morning's walk in a popular area which gets quieter the further away from the reservoir you go is on offer here. After leaving Carsington Water, a leafy old track brings you out beside St Bartholomew's church. From there you climb up until distant views of Staffordshire can be seen. Good views of Carsington Water can then be enjoyed as you head back towards your car, this time passing through a bit more of Hognaston.

There can't be many **Knockerdowns** around and it's all to do with lead mining. Inside the pub there's an explanation of the origin of the name. The pub is ideally placed for Carsington Water and provides some good quality food with specials like Carsington Water fresh whole trout, lamb shank and vegetable and Stilton pasta bake. There is also a children's menu. With good beers such as Pedigree and guests like Timothy Taylor Landlord and Fiddler's Elbow this is a pub worth seeking out. There's a large beer garden so you can sit in the sunshine in summertime and there are also some animals for the children to look at.

Opening times are all day, every day, in summertime.

Telephone: 01629 540209.

Distance: *5½ miles*

OS OL24 The White Peak and Explorer 259 Derby
GR 241516

An undulating walk, though there is likely to be mud in the fields after wet weather to the south of Hognaston.

Starting point: The Carsington Water Visitor Centre.

How to get there: Carsington Water is a couple of miles south-west of Wirksworth. The Visitor Centre is well signposted. To get to the Knockerdown, return to the B5035 and turn right for 150 yards or so.

The Walk

1 From the Visitor Centre walk back towards the entrance and 50 yards before you reach the road bear right up the path (the start of Walk CW4). This takes you parallel to the road to your left. Go as far as possible on this path. Cross the road, heading in the same direction as before between hedges to reach a drive. Turn left downhill through the buildings of Uppertown Farm. Continue as far as you can go until the lane ends. There appear to be three options here: take the middle one to pass through the stile beside a gate. Walk down the right side of the field beyond. Pass through a stile and keep forward. On reaching a track continue down this for 1/4 mile.

2 Ford the stream and turn right. Follow the track round to the left into Hognaston village.

3 With St Bartholomew's church on your left, turn right and 250 yards later, with Longacre on your right, fork left up the tarmac drive. Stay on this as it

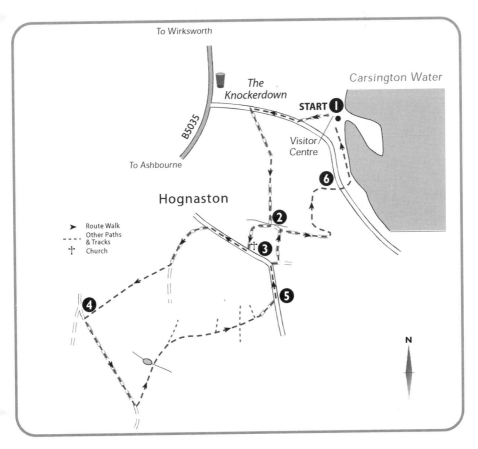

To Wirksworth

The Knockerdown

Carsington Water

B5035

START **1**

Visitor Centre

To Ashbourne

Hognaston

6

> Route Walk
- - - Other Paths & Tracks
† Church

2

†**3**

4

5

N

31

Delightful view of Carsington Water

becomes a gravel track. It levels out and swings left. Cross a cattle grid, pass through a gateway and then cross another cattle grid. Then turn immediately half right to the stile beside a gate 350 yards away at the top of the field. Beyond this, walk forward to the solitary tree ahead. Pass through the stile below it. Head slightly left, aiming 30 yards short of the top left corner. Keep in the same direction across the next field towards the wood.

❹ On reaching a track, with woodland directly in front of you, turn left. This track gives good views towards Carsington Water to your left 1¼ miles away. Stay on the track passing a stone barn on your left and 700 yards later you reach some more buildings on your left. **Immediately** before them, turn left through a small gate. Walk towards the gate at the end of the field. Pass through this and walk beside the hedge on your right, descending to a pond on Parkside Brook. Cross the fence/stile with the pond on your left. Cross another fence/stile and

ascend the field ahead bearing slightly right. As you go, you'll see a farm ahead. Pass through the right-hand of a pair of farm gates. In the field beyond this, walk down to the bottom left corner and pass through the gate there. Keep in the same direction in the more or less square field, crossing the fence at the bottom to come out below an electricity pylon. Then proceed to the bottom right corner of the field with the pylon in it. Walk to the stile beside the gate at the bottom of the next field. Cross the stile and walk up the right side of the hedge on your left. You will be walking on a grassy track. After 300 yards, pass through a gate onto a tarmac track. Proceed along this to reach the old Primitive Methodist Chapel.

❺ Turn left up the village street and 150 yards later turn right along the lane immediately past Ye Olde Forge. Stay on this lane until it swings left 100 yards later. In another 275 yards, turn right downhill when the track splits. Continue downhill, ignoring a horse and cycle route that forks left uphill. Follow the shady path beside the stream on your right and on coming out into the open, turn sharp left uphill beside the woodland. Stay on this path, ignoring the left fork downhill, to come back to the road.

❻ Cross this and turn left back to the Visitor Centre and your car.

Date walk completed:

....

Place of Interest Nearby

A visit to **Wirksworth** is always worthwhile and as time passes you'll get more of an opportunity to use trains that run down the line from Wirksworth to Duffield on the Ecclesbourne Valley line. Telephone: 01629 823076 for more information.

The Hurt Arms

A walk alongside Cromford Canal is always enjoyable and after a mile or so of this a climb up to Crich is rewarded with some stunning views from The Tors. Crossfield paths take you to the village of Fritchley before you return along an unusual path to the start.

Distance: *4³/₄ miles*

OS Explorer 269 Chesterfield and Alfreton
GR 348516

There's a good climb from the canal up to Crich, otherwise a fairly steady walk.

Starting point: The Hurt Arms. Park in their car park, but please make sure you ask first.

How to get there: Amberside is on the A6 just north of Belper. The Hurt Arms is beside the A6 at the point where the A610 joins it.

The Hurt Arms provides excellent meals and is certainly very popular judging by the number of people who use it. It is also known as 'The Home of Derbyshire Ballooning' as you will see from some of the photographs that are pinned to the wall. There is excellent food on offer whether you want something filling such as medallions of fillet steak, steak and chips, pasta bolognaise or a snack like a toasted sandwich or a warm baguette.

Opening times are 11 am to 11 pm everyday (10.30 pm Sunday). Food is served 12 noon to 2.30 pm and 5 pm to 8.30 pm Monday to Friday; 12 noon to 4 pm and 5 pm to around 8.30 pm Saturday and Sunday.

Telephone: 01773 852006.

The Walk

1 From the Hurt Arms, turn left along the A6 for 250 yards. Turn right up Chase Road. On reaching the canal turn left alongside it for one mile. Climb up to the road and cross the canal. Then walk forward for 15 yards or so and follow the track as it rises uphill to the left. After 600 yards, immediately past a 6 ft high wall on your right, climb up the short, but steep, footpath leading to Chase Cliffe. Turn right at the road for 100 yards. Then turn left along the drive of the farm. Keep on the right side of this and the right side of the two fields beyond. Walk on the left side of the third field.

2 Pass through the stile and walk forward into the housing estate. Bear right along the road until 100 yards later, at the end of Chase View, you should swing left for just under 200 yards to reach the end of Bulling Lane.

3 With a grass island on your left, turn right downhill towards Crich marketplace. Keep right, then turn right up Sandy Lane. Beyond Crich Reading Room ignore the path on the left to Sun Lane but 30 yards later take the steps on the left up to the grassy open area. This area marks the Golden and Diamond Jubilees of Queen Victoria. Walk parallel to the road on your right to reach a stone squeezer stile. Pass through this and follow the path beyond. Marvellous far-reaching views open out on your left from this area known as The Tors. When you enter an open field pass through a kissing gate on your left and descend the steps. Keep on down these to reach a road with Torpoint on your left. Turn

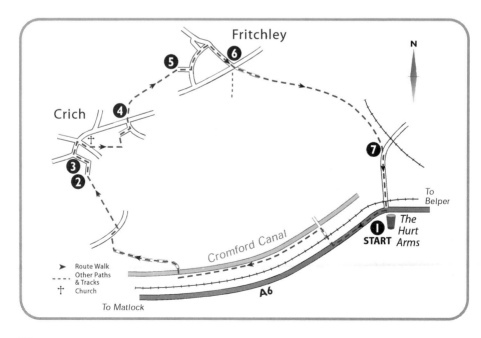

Walking down from The Tors at Crich

5 On reaching a road, head forward on the lower level. Subsequently ignore a lane leading up to the right. Proceed until you reach Church Street. Turn left down to the centre of Fritchley, with a number of grass islands. Turn right here and right again up the road leaving the village almost as quickly as you entered it.

6 You reach a main road 250 yards later. Cross this carefully and walk along the fairly level, wide path in front. Subsequently ignore a path forking right and then one turning sharp left. After this ignore a path to the right, part of the Cromford Canal footpath. On reaching the works bear left and follow the path. Stay on this all the way back to the A610.

7 Turn right here back to the Hurt Arms.

right here, bearing left 100 yards later, by the old chapel, to reach the main road.

4 Cross the road and turn right. Then turn left down the stony track 20 yards later. After 80 yards pass through the squeezer and walk down the left side of the field. In the second field move slightly away from the wall on your left to pass through a stone squeezer – there might be a fence which you have to pass through before this. Proceed along the left side of the next three fields before crossing a sixth field, heading to the left side of the redbrick houses.

Date walk completed:

Place of Interest Nearby
Back up in Crich the **Tramway Museum** is a pleasant way to unwind after your walk and pub stop. There is also a woodland walk and a sculpture trail. Telephone 0870 75 87267 for further information.

Shirley
The Saracen's Head

The walk, starting in Shirley, visits the lovely village of Rodsley where St Ralph Sherwin, the first martyr of the Venerable English College, was born. The 12th century church of St Chad, Longford, is also passed as you follow part of the Bonnie Prince Charlie Walk, that commemorates the 17-mile route that the Stuart prince took from Ashbourne to Derby in 1745.

Distance: *5½ miles*

OS Explorer 259 Derby
GR 219416

This route follows some underused paths so take care to follow the directions carefully.

Starting point: The Saracen's Head. Park in the pub car park, if you intend to visit the pub afterwards. If you are there early, park in front of the pub.

How to get there: Follow the signs for Shirley from the A52 as you head for Ashbourne from Derby. You can't miss the Saracen's Head.

The Saracen's Head is a favourite pub of mine, being a typical village pub, with a nice mix of locals and visitors, including walkers. There's a good choice of food, such as steak and kidney pie, lasagne and chicken Kiev. There is also a variety of beers, including Bass, Pedigree and a guest such as Black Sheep.

Opening times are 12 noon to 3 pm and 7 pm to 11 pm.

Telephone: 01335 360330.

The Walk

❶ From the Saracen's Head walk down the lane following the sign for Rodsley. At a second junction still follow the Rodsley road and after 200 yards fork left along the narrow lane following the Bonnie Prince Charlie Walk. Follow this tarmac drive for 500 yards. Ignore the driveways swinging left to the properties of Wormsley on the left. Stay on the bridleway. When the track swings left into a field, keep forward on the grassy bridleway. Stay on this for some distance. After walking between hedges you come out in the open. Keep forward along the left side of the field. Ignore a path across the bridleway. Walk along the left side of Coppice Plantation. Ahead to your right is Longford church amongst the trees.

❷ On reaching a track forking right towards the church, keep forward through a gate along the Bonnie Prince Charlie Walk. Follow the fence on your left until it bears away to the left. Keep

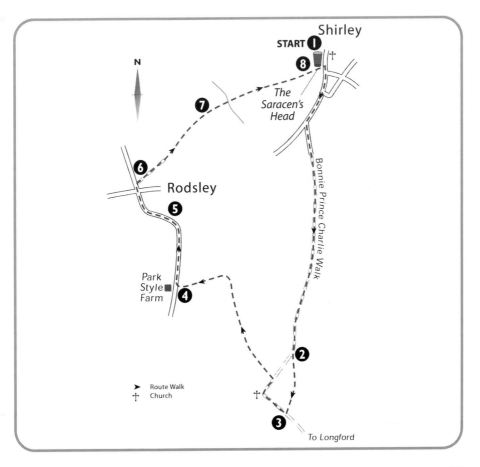

The plaque commemorating St Ralph Sherwin in Rodsley

forward across the field to the bridlegate ahead.

❸ The Bonnie Prince Charlie Walk bears left along the drive. You turn right towards the church. Longford Hall is next to it. Keep to the right of the church heading for the redbrick farm buildings and the clock in the gable end of the building facing you. Swing right at the buildings, walking straight forward keeping the brick buildings on your left. On reaching the last building/structure turn left along a track running alongside various buildings on your left. Where the track splits at the end of the buildings keep forward with a hedge on your left. You reach a wood on your left, 200 yards later. Stay beside this to enter another field. Here you should bear right, away

from the wood, walking up the right side of the field on a track. Stay in this field for 650 yards passing another wood on your right as you go. Leave the field through a gateway, turning left immediately over a stile. Walk up the left side of the field beyond. There may be no sign of a *walked* path but this *is* a public path even if you can't see it. Pass through the gate at the end of the field and head along the track beyond towards Park Style Farm.

❹ Turn right along the lane [Sustrans route 68]. Pass two properties noting the 'slang' beyond the second one. A 'slang' is a long narrow enclosure running alongside a lane from a cottage. These hedges are full of flowers in summertime. A dip in the lane brings you to Compton. Proceed until you enter Rodsley.

5 The road swings left into this attractive village. Keep forward passing French Horn Cottage which used to be the local pub. You pass Rodsley House before reaching the crossroads. The route keeps forward here but on the left is the memorial to St Ralph Sherwin, born in Rodsley in 1550. He became a priest and after being imprisoned and tortured was charged with high treason and executed in 1581.

6 Just beyond the crossroads turn right down the track. Stay on this for just under 400 yards. This is Cow Lane, along which cattle walked down to the fields. At the end of the track, pass through a gate, proceeding down the right side of the field beyond. Pass through another gate and walk up the right side of the next field. Walk up the right side of a third field where the ridge and furrow workings are very clear. In the fourth field keep forward parallel to the hedge on your right. After 80 yards there should be a stile to your left and one to your right. Keep forward bearing a touch to your right into the bottom right corner of the field you're in. Cross the stile here.

7 Pass through the poplars, walking along the right side of the marshy area ahead. Cross a bridge 15 yards upstream from the point where the fence/hedge reaches Shirley Brook. Cross a stile a few yards later. Bear *slightly* left across the ground ahead, crossing a track and rising up a bank to a small clump of holly trees, in which there's a stile! Walk up the right side of the field beyond. Climb a stile in the far right corner of the narrow field after this. Turn left immediately beyond, walking up the left side of the field. At the top of this field, cross a stile by the gate facing you, ignoring one on the left.

8 Beyond the gate, walk up the track keeping to the left of the brick building and with a thatched house to your left. Swing right in front of a beech hedge before bearing left to come back to the pub on your right.

Date walk completed:

....

Place of Interest Nearby
There is a lot to be said for visiting the historic town of **Ashbourne**. There are plenty of interesting buildings including the 13th century St Oswald's church with its 212 ft spire. Telephone Ashbourne Tourist Information Centre on 01335 343666 for further information.

West Hallam
The Newdigate Arms

Just to the west of Ilkeston there is a fascinating area incorporating the Nutbrook Trail and Shipley Country Park that cries out to be explored. Today you get that chance. Enjoy the lovely countryside and all the wildlife though be warned: at Straw's Bridge a little bit of bread for the not-so-wild wildfowl wouldn't go amiss!

Distance: *6³/₄ miles*

OS Explorer 260 Nottingham
GR 442421

A fairly level walk on good paths.

Starting point: The Newdigate Arms. Park in the car park, with the landlord's permission, or at Straw's Bridge and start the walk at [2].

How to get there: Follow the A609 westwards from Ilkeston. Initially you pass Straw's Bridge car park on your right then just over half a mile later the Newdigate on your right, too.

The Newdigate Arms is a good place from which to start your walk and a good place to finish it, too. With Bass, Pedigree, Greene King IPA and guest beers like Deuchars IPA you won't die of thirst. The menu is wide ranging with old favourites such as sausage, egg and chips, sitting next to Moby Dick (a huge battercrisp cod with mushy peas and fries) as well as hot sandwiches such as Beef McCann (hot roast beef with fried onions and mushrooms). Then there are specials and a carvery on Sundays. The Newdigate also has a good-sized beer garden and a large children's playground.

Opening times food is available from Monday to Thursday 12 noon to 2.30 pm and 5.30 pm to 9 pm. On Friday, Saturday and Sunday from 12 noon until 9 pm (8 pm on a Sunday).

Telephone: 01159 320604

The Walk

❶ From the Newdigate Arms turn left on the main road. Continue beside this for just over half a mile to reach the car park on your left at Straw's Bridge.

❷ At the far end of the car park walk round the pond keeping this on your left. Take the first right to join the Nutbrook Trail. Turn left to walk alongside the brook, on your left, which will be running downstream towards you. Stay on the tarmac trail ignoring a track on the right. Stay on the trail as it passes a second pond to your left, then a third one to your right. Pass under an old railway bridge. A mile later, after ignoring a couple of tarmac paths to the housing estates, the trail reaches a point under some electricity lines. Ignore a track to the left here. Stay on the Nutbrook Trail following the sign for Shipley Hill. You should now be walking towards the Adventure Park where screams of delight may be audible. The trail winds left to bring you to a T-junction with a derelict brick building to your left.

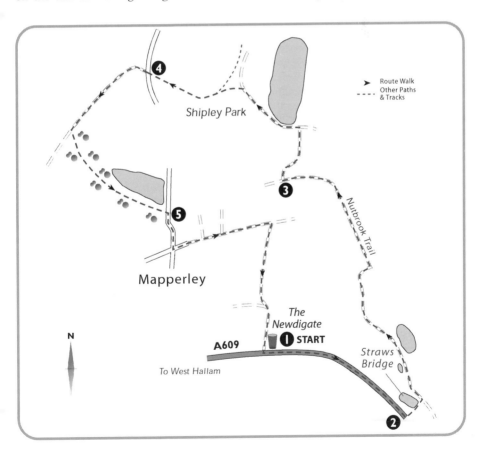

Wildfowl at Straws Bridge

❹ Cross the road, bearing slightly right, to follow the bridleway for 'Mapperley Res.' Some ¹/₂ mile later you reach John Wood. Ignore the gate on your left. In 40 yards turn left through a gap to follow the path through the trees. At the first path junction turn left over a footbridge then sharp right 30 yards later to cross another, wider, footbridge. Bear left 8 or 9 yards later and where the path forks, take the right fork. This brings you to fields on your right. Keep forward now to a lane.

❸ Turn right, signed 'Shipley Park' and 'Heanor'. Pass Paul's Arm, a wetland area for threatened wildlife and at the next T-junction turn left for a good view of Shipley Lake to your right. Beyond the lake the trail stays beside the fence but you fork left up a gravel path rising uphill ahead of you. This brings you to a stone marking the opening of Shipley Country Park on the 26th May 1976. Keep forward between the wall and a gate and pass Nottingham Lodge on your left. There's a nice spot with a seat hereabouts giving a marvellous view towards Heanor across the fields. At the end of the wall keep forward along the drive dropping downhill before walking alongside another wall to pass Derby Lodge on your left.

❺ Turn right up into Mapperley. Turn left at the crossroads into Coronation Road. Follow the public 'bridleroad' for Ilkeston. Ignore a couple of tracks to the left. On reaching a track heading right, take this. Pass Head House Farm, going down the concrete driveway. Ignore a stile on your left to pass under the disused railway bridge. Keep forward along the track between a couple of houses. Stay on this, rising gently. As it levels out turn left then almost immediately right up the tarmac lane. This brings you back to the Newdigate Arms on the main road, the A609.

Date walk completed:

....

Place of Interest Nearby

After visiting the Newdigate Arms continue westward on the A609. Just over half a mile later, on the south side of the road, is the **Bottle Kiln Gallery**, a rare building and well worth a visit as it also has a small shop, a quiet garden and a buttery where you could perhaps have a coffee after you've looked around. Telephone: 01159 329442.

The Mundy Arms

Many of us will have driven through Mackworth without being aware of what lies just to the north of the A52. This walk seeks to address this and if it is the first time you've walked here I will be surprised if you're not impressed when you see the gatehouse of Mackworth Castle for the first time.

The **Mundy Arms** is a very likeable pub, part of a chain, where they have got it just right and there's a good atmosphere. The pub is open all day so there should be no problem having to get there for a certain time. There is plenty of choice with snacks, including rustic knot rolls, hot hobs (a crusty baguette with hot filling of gammon and melted cheese – and other fillings) and also specials: grilled sturgeon being one! There is a good choice of beers, too, with Directors, Pedigree, John Smith and Guinness, plus guests such as Abbot Ale and Bombardier.

Opening times are Monday to Saturday from 11 am to 11 pm; Sunday from 12.30 pm to 10.30 pm.

Telephone: 01332 824254.

Distance: 4¼ miles

OS Explorer 259 Derby
GR 313376

A short, fairly level, walk.

Starting point: The Mundy Arms. Use the car park as long as you ask permission or you can park near Markeaton Park.

How to get there: Follow the A52 westward out of Derby. The Mundy Arms is on the left beside the main road. Turn into the car park immediately beyond the pub.

The Walk

❶ From the Mundy Arms cross the A52 and turn right. Immediately past the Mackworth Hotel turn left along a short driveway, which forms part of the Bonnie Prince Charlie Walk. At the end of the drive, pass through a wooden kissing gate. Walk down the left side of the field beyond. Turn right at the lane.

❷ Where the lane bends right, turn left on the path towards the church. Swing right in front of this keeping the churchyard on your left. At the end of the churchyard bear left to reach another kissing gate. Pass through this and walk alongside a hedge on your left. Keep forward when the hedge ends, heading towards the University building a mile away. The path then runs alongside a hedge on your right. Pass through a gap into the next field where the Bonnie Prince Charlie Walk runs between parallel hedges. Pass through another gap proceeding along the farm track ahead to reach a road. On the bend here cross carefully and walk along the footpath with the road the other side of the hedge on your left. Where the path ends keep forward and follow the road round to the left. Take care here! Walk along the pavement to cross Mackworth Brook. Subsequently pass a car park for Mundy Play Centre, to your right.

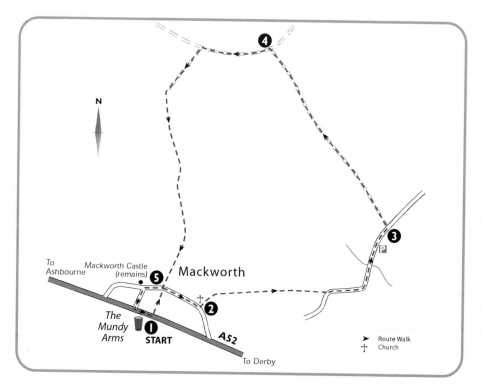

The gatehouse of Mackworth Castle

❸ Just beyond the car park turn left along the tarmac bridleway. Stay on this for 500 yards to reach Stones Farm. Keep the buildings on your left, staying on the bridleway as it becomes a stony track. The heart of Derby is just two miles behind you. About 400 yards beyond Stones Farm ignore a track bearing left into the fields. Keep on the track you're on. Immediately beyond an oak tree ignore a path forking left across the field.

❹ On reaching a tarmac driveway turn left uphill. This driveway bears round to the right and represents your only real 'climb' of the walk. Join this driveway and after 600 yards turn left along another driveway towards Lower Vicarwood. This is just a footpath though, not a bridleway. As you proceed Derby University will be visible to your left with Derby Cathedral to its right – a nice contrast between ancient and modern. As the driveway enters the farmyard resist the temptation to follow it. Immediately before the farmyard, bear left to cross a stile by a gate, with a pond to your left. Walk down the left side of the first two fields and the third field too, heading directly towards a water tower a mile away. Pass through a stile in the corner of the third field and keep on the left side of the fourth and fifth field. Cross Mackworth Brook, this time by a wooden footbridge. Walk 120 yards or so down the left side of the field beyond crossing a stile to walk down the right side of the field ahead. After 75 yards pass through a stile on your right and follow the hedged path to the lane.

❺ Turn right here for 300 yards to reach Gold Lane on your left. This sunken lane leads back to the Mundy Arms. Before you rise up it though, keep ahead to have a look at the remains of Mackworth Castle. The gatehouse forms an impressive entrance to more modest properties beyond it.

Date walk completed:

....

12 *Melbourne*
The Blue Bell Inn

From Melbourne you walk along a path that passes through a cemetery to reach Kings Newton. Then an old track way leads you to Swarkestone Bridge, an ancient monument that used to cross the marshland that was hereabouts. A path then leads between gardens into Stanton by Bridge before you enter some lovely woodland as you steadily make your way back to the start.

The Blue Bell Inn is owned by Shardlow Brewing Company so you will be able to try some different beers and I confess I have sampled them all! Reverend Eaton's, Golden Hop, Narrowboat and Melbourne Mild are all worth trying but don't overdo it if you're driving, of course. There's usually a guest from another brewery available too. You can also get food here but the beer's the novelty. It is a cosy and friendly pub and they also have a barbecue going in summertime, weather permitting.

Distance: 6½ miles

OS Explorer 245 The National Forest
GR 389251

Nothing too strenuous, though one or two of the paths are slightly underused.

Starting point: The Blue Bell Inn. Park in the vicinity of St Michael's church, Melbourne.

How to get there: Follow the A514 south of Derby, follow the sign for Melbourne town centre. Go left at the Market Place and down into Church Street. The Blue Bell is on your left; the church on your right.

Opening times are Monday to Saturday 11 am to 11 pm and Sunday, from 12 noon to 10.30 pm. Food is available Wednesday to Sunday from 11 am to 2 pm and from 7 pm to 10 pm.

Telephone: 01332 865764.

The Walk

1 With your back to the Blue Bell turn left downhill before turning left again along Castle Street. Stay on this. Bear right at a large grass triangle nearly 500 yards later into Station Road. Turn left on a path immediately before Blakemore Avenue. Then turn right beyond house 85. Keep straight forward for 250 yards (passing to the right of house number 27) to enter a cemetery. Still keep forward as the path heads away from the graveyard. Where this path forks, fork left alongside a hedge on your right and 250 yards later you reach King's Newton.

2 Turn left for 130 yards, turning right down a track at Ye Olde Packhorse. Pass Holy Well. Stay on this old track for 1¼ miles. Bear left when you reach Meadow Side.

3 Take the right fork to reach the A514. Swarkestone Bridge is to your right. Keep straight forward across the A514 to find a stile in the 'scrub'. Turn left up the left side of the field beyond. Keep forward on the path through the gardens bearing right when there's nowhere else to go before bearing left after a few paces to cross a stile onto the road.

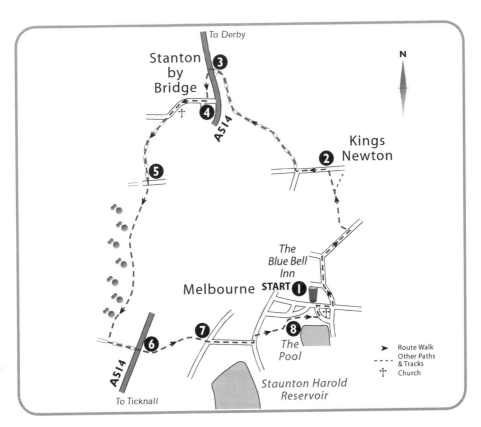

47

Trig point explaining the origin of the bridleway

❹ Turn right through Stanton-by-Bridge. Stay on this road for half a mile passing the church. Ignore all paths to left and right. Continue along the road *beyond* the last building of Stanton, which is a farm, on your right. Keep forward along the stony track, when the road bends right uphill. This levels out between hedges. You reach a drive leading to an isolated property to your right.

❺ Pass through the gate ahead. Walk towards the far right corner of the first field. People seem to walk around the right edge of this field though the legal line of the footpath goes directly across it. Walk on the right side of the second, third and fourth fields, though 150 yards into the fourth field turn right over a

footbridge into the wood. Turn left in the wood keeping in the same direction as before. Keep left until you join a gravel track. Turn left out of Robin Wood to follow a track forming part of the Reservoirs Walk. You should pass under a mast on your left. On the right is Vee's Wood and 450 yards later you reach a road. About 60 yards before it there's an old trig point in the hedge on your left with a plaque on it telling you something about the area.

❻ Cross the road heading along the left side of the hedge, bearing left in this field as the hedge does so. Pass through a gap in the bottom corner of the field. Keep forward to descend the bridleway between a hedge and a fence with St Brides Farm on your left. Pass through to the other side of the hedge continuing in the same direction towards the bottom right corner of the field. Bear left to the bottom left corner though before you get there. In the next field, walk forward, towards the buildings ahead. On your left is Smith's Wood, part of the National Forest. Pass to the left of a breeze-block building proceeding on the tarmac drive beyond.

7 Cross a road when you reach it descending Robinson's Hill. At the T-junction 650 yards later turn left at the Melbourne Arms. Pass through a stile on the right opposite house number 82. Aim for the wall ahead. Proceed alongside it on your left into a second field. Bear left at a hedge corner to come out on a road in Melbourne.

8 Turn right down the road. At the National School, erected in 1822, keep forward down the 'No entry' road. Turn right in front of Vale House through a short 'tunnel' to reach Melbourne parish church. Keep right of the church to reach the entrance before turning left beyond it.

Date walk completed:
....

Place of Interest Nearby
A couple of miles south-west of Melbourne is **Calke Abbey**. Another National Trust property, this is a house with a difference – the result of collecting many artefacts over a number of years. There is also a park and gardens. Telephone: 01332 863822.

13 *Coton in the Elms*
The Queens Head

This walk offers a chance to explore the patchwork of new woods that are part of the National Forest. Take your OS Map as this area is changing all the time. This woodland walk should become an even better one as the years pass by.

The Queens Head is apparently the most landlocked pub in Britain. Parts of it date back to the 16th century and it's quite a find for someone like me from the Derbyshire Dales. Pedigree is available as well as guest beers such as Black Sheep Bitter. The food is good and I particularly enjoyed my steak pie though there's much more to choose from.

Distance: 6¼ miles

OS Explorer 245 The National Forest GR 248152

A fairly level walk with no testing sections. Take care following the directions though.

Starting point: The Queens Head. If using the pub car park, please ask first or use the small Woodland Trust car park at [2].

How to get there: Coton is five miles south of Burton upon Trent. The pub is on the eastern side of the village.

Opening times are 12 noon to 3 pm and 6.30 pm to 11 pm every day, except Monday when it is closed. Food is available 12 noon to 2.15 pm and 7 pm to 9.15 pm.

Telephone: 01283 762573.

The Walk

1 From the pub car park turn right then left into Mill Street. Keep forward alongside the stream in the village to the main road. Bear forward here. Some 60 yards later, take the Lullington road to the left. Stay on this to reach The Malthouse. Turn left into the Woodland Trust car park immediately after.

2 Take the path directly ahead leading out of the car park, ignoring the path to the right. This takes you into Coton Wood. Keep forward along the path and 150 yards after entering the wood the

path splits. Keep forward ignoring the right fork. Your path then swings left, then right, before straightening out. Turn left when the path forks again. Keep on this path to reach a stile on the left but don't cross it. With your back to this take the middle of the three routes in front of you. Keep straight ahead at the cross-paths. Ignore a 'ride' to the right, then a second one. Keep forward to a stile. Cross it, and the bridge beyond. Walk along the right-hand side of the field for 20 yards. At the hedge corner keep forward in the same direction. Cross a driveway when you reach it. This is part of the Spires and Stiles Walk. Keep in the

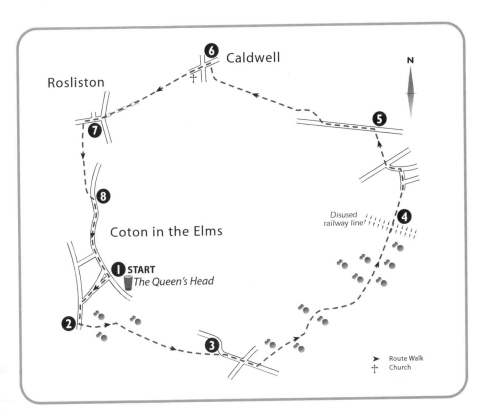

51

Coton in the Elms

same direction in the field beyond the driveway, bearing slightly left in the field beyond that to reach a lane corner.

❸ Turn right. Keep straight ahead at the crossroads for 200 yards. Pass through the gap on your left next to the double-gates into Sisters Wood. Walk forward along the open 'ride', ignoring paths to left and right and 350 yards later cross a stile. Keep forward for 50 yards before bearing slightly right. Then ignore a number of rides to the right then one to the left. Keep forward until, underneath an oak tree, you pass through a gap into Top Wood. Walk up the left side of the hedge rising steadily for 300 yards. Cross a stile and bear right (don't keep forward) alongside a hedge. Drakelow Power Station is away to your left. Head

to the right of the buildings of Park Farm and on reaching a track keep forward past Woodbridge Barn on your left. Cross a stile in front of you keeping forward into the woodland. At the cross-paths turn left heading for Linton. Pass through a gap beside a gate walking down the grassy path beyond. Cross a stile, continue forward, ignoring two rides to the left. Stay beside the hedge on your right. Pass through another gap and proceed with the hedge on your left.

❹ Pass under the disused railway line following the path as it bears half left. Head towards the houses, ignoring paths to left and right. Cross a metal pipe. Pass through a kissing gate and proceed along the lane. Bear left when you reach a road and left at the T-junction. At the next

T-junction, keep forward into the field in front walking along the right side. In the far right corner of the field, bear right to the lane.

❺ Turn left for 400 yards. Pass through a gate aiming for the cooling towers ahead. Pass through a gate in the corner of the field. Head along the left side of the hedge and 100 yards later pass through another gate. Proceed along the line of the electricity poles ahead towards the farmhouse. Walk along the track beyond the gate to the right of an electricity pole in the hedge. In front of the cowsheds, pass through the gates, turning right to reach a lane through another gate.

❻ Turn left into Caldwell. Keep forward at the crossroads along Church Lane. At the church, pass through the middle of three gates along the footpath. Keep down the right side of the wood. Re-enter the National Forest, walking straight forward for 400 yards. Pass through a barrier and head along the track into Rosliston.

❼ Take the path for 'Yew Tree Gardens 5, 7 and 9'. Keep forward through the houses. Cross the stile between houses 18 and 29. Turn left. Walk on the left side of this field and a second one. Keep forward on the right side of field three. Cross two stiles to walk down the left side of Field House and the driveway beyond.

❽ Turn right at the lane into Coton – taking care. Stay on the main road in Coton. Keep forward into Chapel Street to return to the Queens Head.

Date walk completed:

.....

Places of Interest Nearby
Burton upon Trent is a must to visit. **The Trent & Mersey Canal** runs through the town and there's also the **Bass Museum** where you can learn about brewing beer. Telephone: 0845 600 0598.

This is the most northerly Nottinghamshire walk in the book. The Chesterfield Canal flows into the Trent at West Stockwith and there is always something to see in and around West Stockwith Basin. An interesting walk, it passes fascinating buildings and is never far away from water.

Distance: *4¼ miles*

OS Explorer 280 Isle of Axholme
GR 790947

A short level walk

Starting point: The public car park opposite the White Hart Inn.

How to get there: West Stockwith is a little more than 3 miles north-west of Gainsborough on the western side of the Trent. From the A161 just south of Misterton head north-eastwards into West Stockwith. The pub is on the left.

The White Hart is directly opposite the small public car park in West Stockwith so you've no excuses for not going in and enjoying a pint and a pie. It is a regular winner of various CAMRA awards and is usually in the Good Beer Guide. With a policy of having guest beers from different, often local, breweries including Barnsley, Broadstone and Daleside you can be assured of being able to try something a little bit different. There a good selection of food with a traditional three-course meal available on a Sunday but with other bar meals on offer too. There are also sandwiches and burgers. Part of the White Hart dates back 300 years. With a friendly welcome your main problem may be getting in the car park, so get there early!

Opening times are 12 noon to 11 pm every day and food is available from 12 noon to 7 pm (until about 3 pm on Sunday).

Telephone: 01427 890176.

The Walk

1 From the car park turn left over the bridge. Turn right immediately beyond with the River Idle on your right. Where the tarmac lane ends keep forward on the embankment. Stay on this as it leads towards a pair of tall brick chimneys at Misterton Soss. Keep to the right of these. Where the track splits, turn left, signed 'Misterton', and 40 yards later turn right. Keep forward across the field and on reaching the hedge corner, keep forward with the hedge on your left. Through the hedge you may glimpse a pond. On reaching a railway line climb up to and cross it carefully. Take care as the steps may be slippery too.

2 On the far side of the railway line, walk directly across the field aiming just to the right of the church spire three-quarters of a mile away. This brings you to another hedge corner. Again, head forward keeping the hedge on your left. The church spire should still be ahead of you, unless it is lost in mist or fog. At the end of the hedge, keep forward for 6 or 7 yards, then turn right beside a ditch on your left. Stay beside this until you can cross it 50 or 60 yards later by a bridge. From here walk forward heading to the right of the church spire again. Across the field you reach another hedge corner where the path should veer slightly right towards the far end of the field – most walkers seem to proceed with the hedge on their left before (at the end of the field) bearing right for 50 yards to reach a three-fingered metal signpost. Follow the line of the finger pointing to 'Misterton ¼', beside a hedge on your left again! Climb a stile in the field corner, keeping forward beside a red-brick wall, initially, for 60 yards before turning right over a stile on your right to follow a grassy path into Misterton itself.

3 Turn left on the road for the church. Enter the churchyard near the war memorial and take the path to the left of the church. Look out for the gravestone of Annie Turgoose who died in 1913 – I mention this because of the unusual surname! On leaving the churchyard keep forward down the tarmac lane beyond to reach a T-junction.

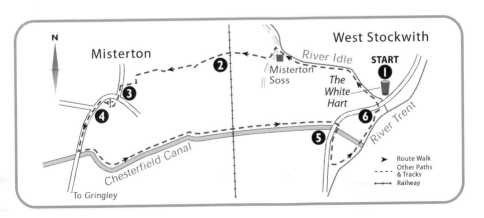

The Chesterfield Canal at West Stockwith

4 Turn left on the road. It soon becomes Gringley Road and 500 yards later passes over the Chesterfield Canal at Cooper's Bridge. Turn left down the steps and walk beside the canal on your right. This is also part of the Trent Valley Way. Stay on this, ignoring a couple of paths to the left. Pass under bridge 81 [dated 1830] then bridge 82. Keep down the left side of the canal at Misterton Top Lock. Pass under the [more] modern bridge 82a. This brings you to Misterton Low Lock. Subsequently bridge 83 is passed under and then the railway bridge [No. 84]. Ahead of you is a long straight stretch of canal. At the end of this don't pass under bridge 85 – rise up to the road with the Waterfront Inn on your left.

5 Cross the bridge and the canal. Proceed right, along the road, passing Bridge House on your right. Turn sharp left, 150 yards or so later, along the bridleway to walk alongside the River Trent to your right. Keep forward to cross the Chesterfield Canal at West Stockwith Lock where the canal water pours into the Trent. Proceed along the grassy embankment beyond. Over the other side of the river is East Stockwith. When the embankment becomes a wall the path rather unceremoniously drops you back down to the road.

6 Turn right back to the White Hart.

Date walk completed:

....

Place of Interest Nearby

Gainsborough is worth exploring, especially **Gainsborough Old Hall**, a medieval manor house in the centre of the town. It has a number of impressive historical connections including with The Pilgrim Fathers. Telephone: 01427 612669.

Langold Country Park 15
The King William IV

This is a fascinating area with an industrial past. The route ventures into Letwell (South Yorkshire) and if you know of a tidier village, let me know. It is rumoured that the St Ledger

Distance: 4³/₄ miles

OS Explorer 279 Doncaster
GR 581866

One climb of sorts on this otherwise level walk.

Starting point: Langold Country Park. To reach the pub return to the A60 and turn north for 1½ miles to Oldcotes. The King William IV is at the roundabout.

How to get there: Enter Langold on the A60 from the south. Turn left into Ramsden Avenue then left immediately into Church Street. Follow the signs for Langold Country Park to the car park.

horse race was originally run just west of Langold. The OS Map shows a large round field a quarter of a mile across.

The King William IV, Oldcotes, is a Brewers Fayre pub and food and drink are available all day. These pubs are clean, friendly and appealing with a wide choice and they add to the 'pub experience' in my estimation. In addition to dishes like gammon and lamb and rosemary suet pudding, there are lighter dishes and salads such as creamy spinach and tomato pasta or spicy vegetable enchiladas. Good beer too with John Smiths, Boddingtons and Trophy Bitter. It's a relaxing place to finish your walking day.

Opening times are from 11 am to 11 pm for drinks and from 11.30 am to 10 pm for food and on Sundays food is available from 12 noon til 10 pm (staying open until 10.30 pm).

Telephone: 01909 730225.

The Walk

1 Walk towards the lake, beyond the car park. Walk round the left side of this. Stay beside it as the path bends right. Look out for the blue waymarks of the Langold Country Walk. Pass the outdoor swimming pool on your left. After 400 yards, just *before* passing under some electricity lines, fork left on a path away from the lake. You'll have to look out for this path as you may miss it initially! This gravel path passes through trees before emerging into the open. Stay on it heading towards the hill ahead, formerly the slagheap of Firbeck Colliery. At the bottom of the hill bear half left more steeply up the hill, amongst youngish trees. The path leaves the trees and moves into the open giving good views. You never reach the top of the hill but drop down towards an old industrial site. On reaching a path running alongside this site, turn right for a third of a mile.

2 On reaching the road, Rotherham Baulk, turn right for another third of a mile. Walk on the grassy verge on the left of the road, which is safer and easier to use.

3 At Buckwood Farm on the right cross the stile by a gate, walking directly away from the road on a track, passing most of the farm buildings to your left. Keep on the track away from the farm. Some 350 yards later there are tracks to left and right, keep forward on the track ahead [beside a wood on your left]. At the far end of the field cross a stile by a gate. Ten

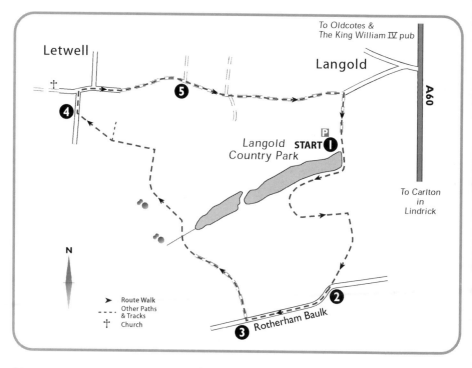

Letwell

To Oldcotes &
The King William IV pub

Langold

A60

Langold **START** ❶
Country Park

To Carlton
in
Lindrick

N

➤ Route Walk
– – – Other Paths
& Tracks
† Church

Rotherham Baulk

Letwell is a delightful village

4 At the road turn right into Letwell, getting on the left side of the road before the bend. Feel free to turn left on Church Lane to have a look round the churchyard and the view beyond. The route follows the main road round to the right. At the left hand bend, keep straight forward along Barker Hades Road. Letwell is a delightful village and you should now walk straight through the older part of it. Look out for the large walnut tree on the right, near the yew tree just before Walnut Cottage. The lane becomes an ash track as you leave the village behind.

yards later cross another step-stile. Keep forward for 20 yards before bearing one-third right across the field ahead, aiming for the far corner. Pass through the trees, crossing a bridge over the stream, to enter the field beyond. Walk across this towards the small wood opposite. On reaching this wood, pass through a gap in the hedge, proceeding with the wood on your left. Continue with the hedge on your left beyond the wood. At the end of the field pass through the hedge, cross a two-plank bridge and turn right beside a ditch for 100 yards. In the corner of the field turn left (in the same field) and proceed alongside the holly hedge on your right for 375 yards. At the corner of the hedge keep forward passing two separate electricity poles ahead of you. At the second one you will see to your right an 18th century brick dovecote. From the second pole the footpath bears half right across the field towards the second electricity pole to the left of the church!

5 On reaching a tarmac driveway keep straight forward. This manicured driveway gives the impression that you're entering National Trust property – but you're not. As the drive swings right for Langold Farm 500 yards later, keep forward down the bridleway. This runs between trees initially, before running down the left side of a field for nearly half a mile. In the bottom corner of the field you enter Dyscarr Wood. Keep forward on the main path/bridleway. This brings you to the entrance to Langold Country Park. Turn right through the gates to get back to your car.

Date walk completed:

....

Places of Interest Nearby
Head south for 1½ miles forking right to visit **South Carlton** church. It may not be open but it's worth walking round the churchyard. For a few weeks in winter visit **Hodsock Snowdrop Garden**. It is two miles south-east of the car park. Telephone: 01909 591204.

The delightful village of Hayton is the starting point for this walk which explores some of the green lanes of Hayton and Clarborough before you walk back along the Chesterfield Canal to the pub.

The **Boat Inn** backs onto the canal so you could sit in the beer garden and watch the

Distance: 4¼ miles

OS Explorer 271 Newark on Trent GR 728852

A level walk with one minor 'climb'.

Starting point: On the roadside in the village south of the Boat Inn.

How to get there: Hayton is on the B1403 north of Clarborough on the A620 to the north-east of Retford.

odd narrowboat go by, or just the world. I have to recommend the carvery which is on offer Sunday lunchtime, it is very good value for money. Sunday is also a busy day, however, because the Boat has such a good reputation. There are filled rolls, hot and cold baguettes, jacket potatoes and then the main courses with good traditional pub food on offer, in the bar menu. There's cottage pie, steak pie, battered cod, beef or chicken curry, just the sort of thing with which to wind up a walk. The beers are Hardys and Hansons Traditional Mild and hand pulled bitter plus Stones Bitter.

Opening times: Weekdays 12 noon to 3 pm and then 5 pm to 11.30 pm, except Monday when it is closed during the day. At the weekend it is open from 12 noon to 11 pm; 10.30 pm on Sunday.

Telephone: 01777 700158.

The Walk

❶ Walk back to the Boat Inn. Instead of turning left over the bridge and the canal keep straight forward into Burntleys Road. Follow this round to the right after 20 yards or so. This rises gently and is likely to be the most testing part of the walk, such as it is! At a staggered crossroads, turn right along the level track. Continue until you reach a track dropping downhill to the right 400 yards later – ignore this. Continue forward between high hedges. At a crossroads of tracks keep straight across. These are wide tracks, grassy on the whole though sometimes cut up. Some of the hedges around here in late summer are full of sloes, rose hips and elderberries. The section beneath the electricity lines is Lovers Walk. The track narrows and you reach the A620.

❷ Cross this carefully and take the footpath just to the right of where you reached the road. Walk along the bottom side of three fields. In the fourth bear slightly left, alongside a hedge on your right to reach a lane.

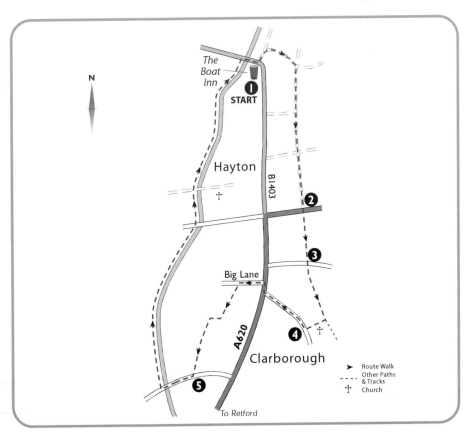

N

The Boat Inn

START

Hayton

B1403

Big Lane

A620

Clarborough

To Retford

Route Walk
Other Paths & Tracks
† Church

A peaceful stretch along the Chesterfield Canal at Hayton

❸ Turn left uphill for 10 to 15 yards before turning right along a path leading directly away from the lane, into the trees. Keep forward for 175 yards or so. Walk along the bottom side of the first field heading straight across a second one. Turn right down the track to the main road though you may wish to walk down through the churchyard, past the church (which is probably not open) to reach the road.

❹ Turn right to the main road then right along this for 100 yards. Turn left down Big Lane and 375 yards along here take the path on the left into a field heading diagonally across this. Climb a stile in the far left corner and turn right for 150 yards, initially alongside a hedge on your right. Turn left towards the gable end of a house just over 400 yards away. As you go you will eventually be walking alongside a hedge on your left.

❺ On reaching the lane in front of Well House, turn right to cross the canal bridge at Bonemill Farm. Walk forward a few yards over the bridge before turning sharp left to reach the canal. Then turn left under the bridge [No. 61]. Stay on the canal to pass the Gate Inn where you also pass under bridge 62. Pass under bridge 63, though if you wish to climb up to the lane and turn right you will reach Hayton church 200 yards later. Back beside the canal, proceed under bridges 64, 65 and 66. Having passed under bridge 66, turn sharp left up to the road before crossing the bridge to reach the Boat Inn.

Date walk completed:

....

Places of Interest Nearby

Drive three miles south and have a look around **Retford**. There are some attractive Georgian houses in the town, a museum and the **Chesterfield Canal**. Retford Tourist Information can be contacted on 01777 860780.

A walk around a power station doesn't sound very inviting but the proof is in the pudding! From Church Laneham with its lovely church you follow lanes and tracks to the foot of Cottam Power Station. A lovely path alongside the cooling towers leads you into Cottam itself before a bridleway takes you to the Trent. Then you follow the embankment all the way back to the start. Take your binoculars because there are a couple of large ponds on the way full of wildfowl.

Distance: *8 miles*

OS Explorer 271 Newark on Trent
GR 813766

A level walk with no climbs except up some ten ft high embankments! If the Trent is in flood you won't be able to do this walk.

Starting point: In Church Laneham near the Ferry Boat Inn. If there is no space, park at Laneham and walk back, along the lane.

How to get there: From the A57 just west of Dunham on Trent head north for one mile for Laneham. Fork right into Laneham and keep right until you reach Church Laneham.

Although it's the **Ferry Boat Inn** sadly there is no ferryboat service across the Trent nowadays. The pub dates back to the 1700s and it's a friendly place where you will be made welcome with a good choice of food from a regular menu but also specials which include Cumberland Sausage ring, Surf and Turf, and beef or prawn curry. The beers include Stones, Worthington, Mansfield Smooth and John Smiths Handpulled. In summer there will be guests like Timothy Taylor Landlord.

Opening times are every day 12 noon to 11 pm (Sunday to 10.30 pm). Food availability in summer is likely to be from 12 noon until about 8 pm, though in winter these hours may be cut down somewhat.

Telephone: 01777 228350.

The Walk

❶ With your back to the Ferry Boat Inn turn left and walk along the lane. Cottam Power Station looms up ahead of you. Beyond the village, when the road turns left, keep forward on the byway directly towards the eight cooling towers of the power station. Stay on this, ignoring paths to right and left. Directly in front of the power station you reach a T-junction of byways.

❷ Turn left. 400 yards later turn right on a path for Cottam, Treswell and Leverton. This runs along the western side of the power station and is surprisingly attractive. Stay on the path for ³/₄ mile until you reach the road at the far end of the power station.

❸ Turn right at the road into Cottam. Pass the entrances into the power station. Stay on the main road crossing a bridge over a railway line. In Cottam pass the Moth and Lantern pub and bear left

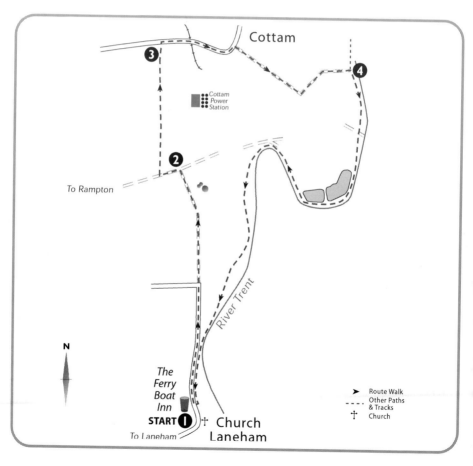

These ponds on the Trent are often full of wildfowl

round the corner. Less than 100 yards later turn right along a bridleway taking you away from the village. This track proceeds between trees for about two-thirds of a mile before swinging left into the open. It subsequently crosses an embankment. Keep straight forward to reach a second embankment with the river immediately beyond. You may have to pass through a small enclosure to get there and you may not see the river until you reach the second embankment.

❹ Turn right along the embankment following the Trent Valley Way, though there may be no waymarks to indicate this. Reach a disused railway line, after 500 yards, and keep to the right of the small archway to climb up to the old line and cross it descending on the far side. Keep forward beyond on the embankment nearest the river. As you proceed, Torksey church and castle are across the river. The Trent begins to bear right in a long bend. You will see a couple of large ponds on your right which are usually full of wildfowl. The causeway between these ponds is a bridleway but take care. Keep following the embankment as it steadily bears right (before it then bends left). You will be heading back towards the power station. Stay on the embankment as it becomes a track between fences. Stay on this for a few yards before leaving it by a stile on the left to get back to the grassy embankment. Continue along this past a pumping station on your right. Pass under a conveyor belt. Keep on the banking for the next mile or so, sometimes near the river sometimes away from it. On reaching Trentfield Farm immediately to your right, stay on the embankment, but halfway along the field beyond the farm descend the steps on your left. This takes you down to the river's edge. Turn right then and follow the path all the way back to the road. Continue back along the road to the pub.

Date walk completed:

_____

The Clumber Park Hotel

A walk of two halves – beginning and ending in the stunning National Trust scenery of Clumber Park and Hardwick village with a middle section on the eastern side of the A614. This is still attractive but much, much quieter.

The Dukeries Tavern is part of the Clumber Park Hotel, which used to be part of the Clumber Estate. Here you'll be made welcome and be able to enjoy light bites, hot baguettes, sandwiches or The Main Event. The latter, featuring dishes such as roasted vegetable lasagne, sirloin steak as well as a selection of curries or penne pasta and garlic bread. With Boddingtons and Flowers IPA available you will soon find your batteries recharged. There is a carvery on Sundays.

Distance: *8 miles*

OS Explorer 270 Sherwood Forest
GR 626747

A fairly level walk but there may be some mud in the woods.

Starting point: The chapel in Clumber Park. You can park at this National Trust property but a fee will be payable unless you're a member.

How to get there: Look out for the 'Clumber Park' signs north of Ollerton on the A1. Enter Clumber Park and two miles later park as near as you can to the chapel.

Opening times are 12 noon to 9.30 pm in summer; 12 noon to 2 pm and 5.30 pm to 9.30 pm in winter.

Telephone: 01623 835333.

The Walk

1 Walk to the chapel, then the lake beyond. Turn left alongside the lake. In 500 yards, a few yards beyond two stone seats surmounted by lions' heads, fork left on a path into the trees. Take the second path on your right (just a few yards beyond a rather indistinct path) bearing right when this joins another from the left. Pass through an arched gate. Follow the gravel track to a pair of low gateposts. Turn right on the path between the wood and the field. Stay on this to enter the wood, still with the lake on your right. Swing left as the lake does and 400 yards later turn right, passing between two lakes to reach a lane.

2 Turn right, then right again off the lane with the lake still on your right. Pass through a parking area. The lake opens out to your right. Just beyond the toilets bear left following the Robin Hood Way, walking through a tarmac parking area

past a farm on your right. Uphill are the houses of Hardwick Village. At a T-junction turn right to a ford. Cross this and 100 yards later turn left into a field. Walk diagonally across this field for half a mile, with Cabin Hill Covert at the top of the field, to reach the far corner. Cross an access drive, and head along a gravel path on the right side of a plantation. This swings left to the entrance of Clumber Park. Turn left to the main road.

3 The Clumber Park Hotel is to your left. Cross the road carefully, heading along the bridleway ahead, on the Robin Hood Way. Keep forward, cross a stile and continue on the track ahead, just inside the wood with fields to your left. Cross a track that leads into the fields, continuing forward. Cross another track. When your track swings left, keep straight forward towards the open ground ahead. At the end of the wood head along the track in front and half

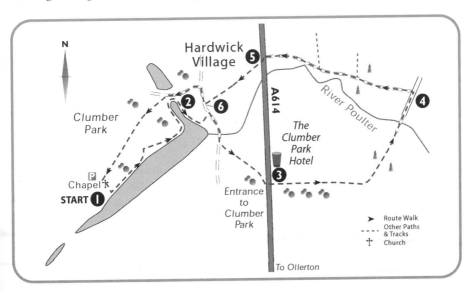

A ford near Hardwick

right is the tower of Bothamstall church. On reaching some electricity lines turn left, still following the Robin Hood Way. Keep forward through the wood. With a gate to your left, bear slightly right to a track to then bear left downhill. Cross the River Poulter. Keep along the track beyond, keeping forward when you reach a lane.

4 Turn left along the driveway to Crookford Farm. Pass most of the farm buildings to your left. Half a mile later, keep forward through the plantation, ignoring a track bearing right at the far end. The grassy track continues ahead. Ignore another track heading uphill, 500 yards later. The bridleway/track swings away from the river to reach the main road.

5 Cross the A614 carefully to re-enter the National Trust property. Follow the path under the trees and on joining a

cycle route from the right, keep forward with the fields on your left. Leave the wood, walking beside a fence on your left. The bridleway wheels right slightly and you walk beside a woodland on your left. Ignore a grassy track through the trees on your left, then a second one. Shortly after, the bridleway passes through the wood. The field beyond this leads into Hardwick village.

6 At the lane turn right past the 20th century houses. Keep forward to the war memorial. Fork left on the road just beyond, descending through lovely woodland. The lane passes between two ponds. Yes, you've been here before! Bear left along the gravel path used before. In the wood, don't turn left, head up the path into the wood. Stay on this main gravel path to reach a crossroads of paths. Turn left and 20 yards later fork right along a wide gravel path to reach a gate with an open area beyond. Cross this following the waymarks heading just right of the chapel. Some 400 yards later you should reach the far left corner of this open area. With the chapel just 200 yards away, head back to your car.

Date walk completed:

Place of Interest Nearby
This is easy! **Clumber Park** itself. Call the National Trust on 01909-544917 for further details about visiting the chapel, kitchen garden and walking around the lake.

The Jug & Glass

One of the longest walks in the book and probably one with the most contrasts. There are lovely woods, including Graves Wood, which is the most impressive bluebell wood I have ever seen. There is also a chance to reflect upon what man was doing in this area 50,000 years or so ago, and you will also have the chance to follow part of the Robin Hood Way.

Distance: 8¼ miles

OS Explorer 270 Sherwood Forest
GR 525705

A long, level walk

Starting point: The car park at GR 525705 (the route is described from here) or in front of the Jug & Glass pub (GR 535704 and start the walk at [9]).

How to get there: Follow the A632 east from Bolsover. In Langwith follow the 'Archaeological Way' car park signs. Park at the first car park near the dismantled railway bridge.

The first thing that strikes you about the **Jug and Glass** is the excellent position it occupies beside the infant River Maun. It's very popular with visitors in good weather as you can imagine. There is plenty of choice on the menu and good Hardys and Hansons beer. Please note: the pub is *very* busy Sunday lunchtime.

Opening times are Monday to Saturday 11.30 am 'until late' (food until 2 pm) and on Sunday from 12 noon to 4 pm, (food served until 2.30 pm), and 7 pm to 10.30 pm.

Telephone: 01623 742283.

The Walk

❶ Walk back to the lane. Turn right. Pass a pond on your left. In 200 yards take the bridleway on your left into the wood. You will soon be walking beside a field to your left.

❷ On reaching another track, turn right along a delightful woodland bridleway. Keep forward where the tracks cross, following the Archaeological Way, then forward at a second 'crossroads'. When the track splits, fork right. At the edge of the wood, the mounds either side of the path are all that remain of the *Park Pale,* the fence that used to surround Scarcliffe

Park, this ancient deerpark. Head across the field towards the line of trees. Bear left in the trees with the millpond down to your right. Stay on this bridleway, turning right uphill on reaching a redbrick house, to enter Whaley (pronounced 'warlee').

❸ Turn left along the road. Then right immediately beyond the Black Horse, for Elmton. Some 120 yards later ignore a road on the right. At Whaley Common turn right at the T-junction for 150 yards. Turn left along the bridleway for half a mile. Just beyond Frithwood Farm, leave the Archaeological Way, turning left along the tarmac lane. In 500 yards cross the stile on your right, walking beside a hedge on your left. Climb onto the disused railway line. Turn left for a few yards then right down the steps. Head straight forward on this path ignoring all paths, left and right. Cresswell Colliery used to be on the right. In 1950, 80 men lost their lives here in one of the worst mining accidents in this country. Some 500 yards after crossing the *old* railway line, cross a bridge over the *current* one. Keep forward to join Morven Street. This subsequently becomes Duchess Street and brings you to the main road.

❹ Turn left then right 50 yards later at the mini-roundabout following the road towards Cresswell Crags. In 400 yards turn right on a path to leave the road and enter the Cresswell Crags area.

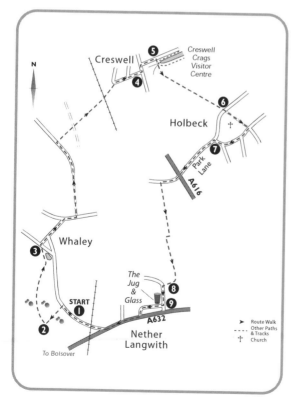

Scarcliffe Park is an ancient deer park

5 You should keep right on the path to leave the Crags almost as soon as you reach them by following the Robin Hood Way. Steps lead up into a field. Proceed along the path in the field. To your right is Cresswell. Bear left rising to the top of the field, then aim for a stile at the left end of the fence between two woods. Beyond this walk to the far left (bottom) corner of the field 300 yards away. Continue along the left side of the next field. Keep forward between woods either side of you. Cross a stile, continuing forward, across another stile. You should now have a hedge on your right. Enter another field, still beside the hedge. At the end of this field continue between hedges, then along a drive, to reach the road in Holbeck.

6 Turn left, then almost immediately right along the Robin Hood Way, through an avenue of trees. In 250 yards you reach Holbeck church. Continue along the lane to a crossroads. Turn right then right again after 175 yards, rising uphill. At a T-junction turn right to the road 100 yards away.

7 Then turn left along Park Lane, though it may not be signed. Half a mile later, cross the A616. Keep on the outside of the right hand bend. In 200 yards take the path on the left towards Graves Wood across the field. Walk through the left side of this oak woodland. Proceed down the left side of the field beyond. Cross the wall, turn right. Some 100 yards later turn left up to the stile beside the gate 100 yards ahead. Proceed down the sandy drive before bearing right to a road.

8 Turn left to the Jug and Glass.

9 Turn right in front of the pub. Proceed with the stream on your left for 300 yards. The road swings left to take you to the A632. Turn right for 200 yards, then right again, then almost immediately left into the park. Stay beside the stream on your left for 200 yards to reach a road. Turn right back to your car.

Date walk completed:
....

Place of Interest Nearby
Creswell Crags should be visited either on the walk, adding to your mileage, or afterwards. Man lived here over 50,000 years ago and it is well worth visiting the informative website at www.creswell-crags.org.uk before you go or telephone 01909 720378 for details.

The Forest Lodge Hotel

Sherwood Forest, Robin Hood, the Major Oak and the Archway House are all in the melting pot on this fascinating walk. The first three you will have heard of, but the fourth may be something of a surprise to many.

Distance: 5¼ miles

OS Explorer 270 Sherwood Forest GR 627676

A level walk.

Starting point: The Sherwood Forest Visitor Centre Car Park. For the Forest Lodge Hotel turn right from the Visitor Centre into Edwinstowe. The hotel is on your left as you enter Edwinstowe.

How to get there: Follow the A6075 from Mansfield into Edwinstowe. Turn left at the crossroads along the B6034. Half a mile later turn left into the Sherwood Forest Visitor Centre Car Park.

The **Forest Lodge Hotel** dates back to the 18th century and food is available all day. There is a bar as well as a restaurant. The bar food is all reasonably priced and you can expect to choose from dishes like shepherds pie, steak pie, roast turkey dinner, gammon steak with pineapple or egg. Bear in mind it can get very busy at the weekend and over the Bank Holidays so get there early to claim a seat!

Opening times are 11.30 am to 2.30 pm (or 3 pm depending on how busy they are) and in the evenings from 5.30 pm to 11 pm.

Telephone: 01623 824443.

The Walk

❶ From the car park follow the signs to the Visitor Centre/Major Oak. Directly in front of the Visitor Centre bear left. A few yards later ignore the Greenwood Walk. Follow the fenced gravel path passing various old gnarled oak trees. The path forks again, keep forward for the Major Oak. Cross a public bridleway. A sign tells you the Major Oak is five minutes walk away. You then reach this old tree, probably the most famous one in the country, if not the world. It is 23 tons in weight, 33 ft all the way round and 800 years old.

❷ Continue round the fencing surrounding the tree to pick up the green bow and arrow waymarks for the Robin Hood Way. Follow the direction of the arrow by turning left along a gravel path. Proceed on this route. Stay on the clear gravel path. On reaching an angled 'crossroads', take the bridleway to the right, not the sharp right turn though. The path you're following is 6 ft wide and runs alongside a conservation area at

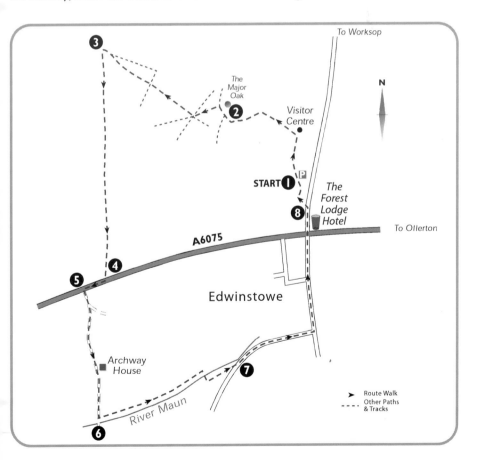

73

The venerable Major Oak

present. Ignore all minor paths running off it. Half a mile from the 'angled' crossroads take the left fork, when the bridleway forks. After 50 yards cross the grassy path that crosses the bridleway, which is now more grass than gravel. At a point where a number of paths converge, keep forward to the open area with a wider stony track 50 yards beyond.

3 On reaching this stony track turn left to follow another bridleway. Keep straight ahead for 1¼ miles, ignoring various bridleways to your left as you go.

4 Immediately before the A6075 bear right along the bridleway with the road just to your left.

5 A little further on, cross the road carefully and follow the bridleway, a tarmac driveway, to Clipstone. Ignore a rough track to your left. You are following the Robin Hood Way again. The bridleway reaches a field on your right before entering the trees again.

Before you know it you reach Archway House, a most impressive and unusual property. Twenty years ago this area was open ground and the house easier to see. Continue along the track beyond it until you reach a bridge over the River Maun.

6 Do not cross the bridge but turn left. Follow the bridleway beside the river on your right for 250 yards. It then forks, the public right of way keeping forward, with open fields on your left. For 400 yards you're walking beside the fields on your left with a wood on your right. Then the bridleway runs on the left side of a long field for 400 yards with Edwinstowe ahead. Turn right to cross an agricultural bridge, ignoring another bridleway to the left. The bridleway crosses the River Maun. Stay beside the river, on your left, for nearly half a mile.

7 At the road turn left. Some 400 yards later at the main road turn left and walk straight through Edwinstowe to the crossroads. Go straight across and rise gently, passing the church to your left.

8 At the edge of Edwinstowe turn left at Forest Corner and immediately right following the track which runs along the right side of a cricket ground. At the far side of this follow the signs for the Visitor Centre and the Major Oak. In 60 yards bear right along a path for the Centre.

Date walk completed:
....

Place of Interest Nearby
A couple of miles south of Edwinstowe is **Rufford Country Park** which contains the ruins of an abbey plus gardens and a lake. Telephone: 01623-822944.

The Dovecote Inn

Laxton is well known for its medieval field system. This walk, though, explores the less well known north-eastern side of the village before looping round to come back into Laxton, passing the remains of the castle and the ancient 'tofts' that can still be seen running down towards the old farmsteads.

Distance: 3¼ miles

OS Explorer 271 Newark on Trent
GR 724671

A short level walk which can be muddy after wet weather.

Starting point: The Dovecote Inn. Park in the Visitor Centre car park behind the pub or, if it is full, on the streets thereabouts.

How to get there: Laxton lies 3 miles or so east of Ollerton.. As you drive through Laxton on the main road you will eventually reach the pub.

The Dovecote is an inviting pub with excellent food on offer. In addition to the more common dishes, such as scampi, baguettes and steak in Guinness pie, there are also more unusual dishes like Thai vegetable curry and steak rossini. With Mansfield Smooth, Banks's and Pedigree with guests such as Bombardier and Black Sheep there are some good beers too. You can even stay at the Dovecote as they do bed and breakfast or you can camp on the grass at the back of the Visitor Centre car park.

•

Opening times are Monday to Saturday 11.30 am to 3 pm and 6.30 pm to 11 pm. Sunday 12 noon to 3 pm and 7 pm to 10.30 pm.

Telephone: 01777 871586.

The Walk

❶ From the Dovecote Inn, turn left down Main Street passing the pinfold almost immediately. There is a map of the Laxton Estate in the pinfold. Turn left shortly after, over a stile between hedge and fence. Ascend the path and climb a stile into the field walking up the right side of this. Cross into a second field but after seven or eight yards cross a stile on your right. Turn left beyond, walking along the left side of the third field, before passing through a gap. At a crossroads of paths continue straight forward keeping on the right side of a broken fence as you go. Take care, there might be a few nettles hereabouts in summer! After 60 or 70 yards, keep forward along the grassy path, known as Stony Baulk. On reaching a couple of hawthorn trees directly in front of you, pass them and continue along the grassy path beyond.

❷ This brings you to a hedged track known as Wood Lane. Turn right along this and stay on it until 600 yards later you're no longer walking between hedges but along the left side of a field. Turn left through a gap in the hedge and walk directly up that field towards the single oak tree ahead, keeping parallel to the hedge to your left. On reaching the tree bear one third left to the far left corner of the field which is just to the right of the wooden electricity pole. Look out for the Scarlet Pimpernel underfoot in late summer. In the field beyond turn left for 20 yards then right heading for the corner of the wood 300 yards away – to the left of this, in the distance, is the spire of Tuxford church and to the left again is Tuxford Windmill. At the corner of the wood, turn left along the bridleway. On reaching a hedge, 250 yards later, turn left beside it and 150 yards after turn right along the bridleway, with the hedge on your right, to reach a lane 500 yards further on.

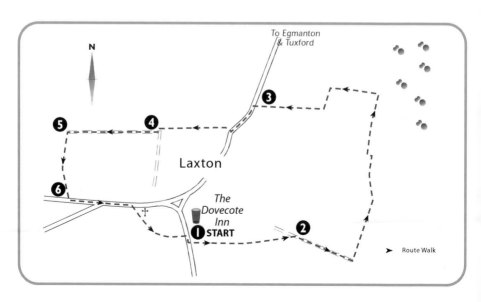

The churchyard of St Michael's church, Laxton

❸ Turn left along the lane and 350 yards later on the right is a pair of gateways. Pass through the right hand one and bear left alongside the hedge on your left. Keep on the left side of the second field too. At the end of the second field pass onto the other side of the hedge keeping in the same direction. At the end of the third field pass through a gate on your right and bear left maintaining the direction in which you were heading before. In this field there are a number of earthworks and when you pass through the bridlegate at the end of the field you will see to your right what remains of 11th century Laxton Castle. The interpretation panel describes it as the *'best preserved and possibly finest motte and bailey'* in Nottinghamshire.

❹ With your back to the old castle bear right along grassy Hall Lane, though it isn't signed at the time of writing. Don't walk down the grassy lane towards a house! On the left as you proceed are the 'tofts' which were, and still are to some extent, long narrow fields which each farm on the main street had stretching behind them. This 'lane' seems neglected now, not particularly well used but 500 years ago it would have presumably been very much busier.

❺ At the end of Hall Lane, cross a stile [ignoring a stile to your right] and cross another stile on your left. Walk down the right side of the field you enter bearing slightly left as you near the village and the field narrows. Climb a stile onto the tarmac lane.

❻ Turn left along this. At the junction bear left towards 12th century St Michael's church. Enter the churchyard and follow the path to the right of the church. At the porch there is a millstone from the mill which collapsed nearby in 1916 and to the left of it an old sundial. Follow the path between the sundial and the millstone to reach the far right corner of the churchyard. Pass through a gap to leave the churchyard and bear left down to the main street ignoring a path to the left as you proceed. This brings you back to the Dovecote Inn.

Date walk completed:

....

ased on the lovely red-brick village of Collingham I recommend you take your binoculars with you as there is usually plenty to see on this circuit. There are also some unusual clapper gates on the Trent embankment before you get back to Collingham itself.

Distance: 6¼ miles

OS Explorer 271 Newark on Trent
GR 832624

Another walk without a hill to be seen.

Starting point: The Grey Horse. Park here, having first asked the landlord's permission.

How to get there: Collingham is north of Newark on the A1133. The Grey Horse is at the northern end of the village.

The Grey Horse is a welcoming village pub, which still organises traditional pub games. There is a wide range of food including burgers, bacon cobs, sandwiches, jacket potatoes and more substantial items like beef and onion pie and cottage pie. Cask beers such as John Smith Cask, Bombardier and Wadsworth 6X are also available.

Opening times are weekdays from 11.30 am to 3 pm; Saturday from 11.30 am to 11 pm; and Sunday from 12 noon to 10.30 pm. Food is available from 12 noon until 2 pm and 5 pm until 8.30 pm Monday to Saturday and on Sundays from 12 noon until 3 pm and 6 pm until 8.30 pm.

Telephone: 01636 892330.

The Walk

❶ Walk away from the A1133. After 350 yards, turn right, immediately beyond Rutland Cottage. Follow the footpath until it bears left then right over a small stream. Walk along the right side of the field beyond for 300 yards before, with a pond on your right, you bear slightly left across the field towards an electricity pylon on the far side of the field beyond the one you're in. Cross a

bridge and turn slightly left in the direction of a red-brick building half a mile away.

❷ On reaching a track turn right. Subsequently follow the gravel track to the right ignoring a grassy hedged footpath in front. Cross the entrance to Besthorpe Quarry 400 yards later. Continue beyond. You now reach a large pond on your left that is full of wildfowl. The track bends to the left. There are

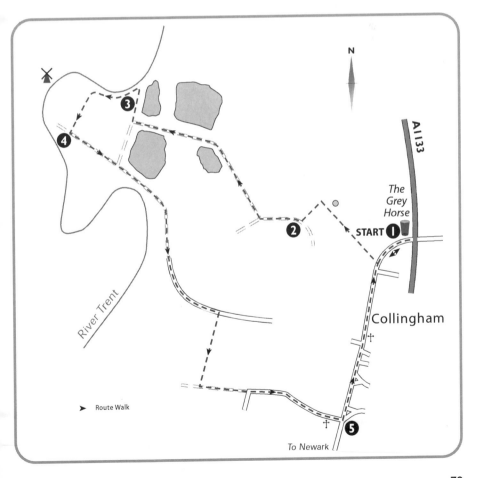

A peaceful corner in Collingham

more ponds to the right and left as you proceed for the next ½ mile. As the track turns left again take a footpath on your right alongside Besthorpe Nature Reserve on your right. Follow this to the River Trent.

❸ Turn left along the embankment. Stay on this passing through an unusual pair of gates. The path leads towards the disused windmill and the impressive church spire of Carlton-on-Trent to its left. The path, still on the embankment, swings left away from the windmill.

❹ On reaching another track turn left. Ignore another track to the left half a mile later. Stay on the track you are on for another mile as it swings right then left, ignoring a number of paths as you go. With the redbrick Ferry Lane Farm 300

yards ahead of you, turn right into a field following a bridleway. Walk beside the hedge on your left. Stay beside this as it becomes a track running between hedges to another track. Turn left here. You are now on the Trent Valley Way, though you may not realise it. You reach Westfield Farm to your right 450 yards later. Keep forward. At the time of writing there are a couple of interesting signposts beside the road here which read 'Wildlife verge do not disturb'. The lane is by now laid with tarmac. Keep forward along it into Collingham. You may wish to visit the church on your right though it may not be open.

❺ At the T-junction turn left. Keep left of the grass triangle to walk along Low Street. Keep on this as it bears left by another grass triangle. Ignore all roads to the right. On reaching All Saints church note the height of the flood in 1795, shown by the church gate. Stay on Low Street to get back to your car.

Date walk completed:

_____

Place of Interest Nearby

Newark Air Museum has a large collection of aircraft. It's a couple of miles north-east of Newark itself. Telephone: 01636 707170.

The Hutt

One third of this walk may be on roadside footways but this gives you an opportunity to enjoy Ravenshead and its surroundings. Most of the route, though, runs through Newstead Park, with its connections with Lord Byron.

The Hutt is the oldest building in Ravenshead and it is a really striking

Distance: 6¼ miles

OS Explorer 270 Sherwood Forest GR 556545

A mid-length flat walk.

Starting point: The Hutt pub. Park in the car park with the landlord's permission.

How to get there: The Hutt is opposite the entrance to Newstead Abbey on the A60 in Ravenshead.

building too, set beside the main road. It is a Chef & Brewer pub, with good food, good beer and a good atmosphere – the sort of pub you want to take a leisurely lunch in. With a wide choice of beers, Directors, Theakstons XB and Best Bitter, plus a guest such as Adnams Broadside, and excellent food, such as beef and melted cheese or tuna crunch with spring onion & celery, sliced tomatoes and melted cheese, I'm sure you'll enjoy your visit. It has not always been a pub mind you. At different times it's been an inn, a rectory, a private residence, a Berni Inn and refreshment rooms! Long may it stay as an excellent pub.

Opening times are 'eight days a week' according to their menu. In other words, 11 am until 11 pm Monday to Saturday, and 12 noon until 10.30 pm on Sunday.

Telephone: 01623 792325.

The Walk

1 Walk to the narrow end of the car park between the A60 and the road into Ravenshead. On the right is The Hollies. Take the footpath to the left of this for St Peter's church. Fortunately not everyone surrounds themselves with high fences, though a lot do, on this path! On reaching Sheepwalk Lane turn left for ½ mile, passing the modern church as you proceed.

2 At the T-junction bear left uphill to reach the traffic lights after 400 yards. Cross the A60 carefully and walk along Kirkby Road. Half a mile later, immediately past the last house on the left, No. 51, turn left and follow the Robin Hood Way. Take a left turn then a right onto the Woodland Trust property.

3 The path runs parallel to a stone wall on the left, just a few yards away. You soon leave the Woodland Trust property and find yourself walking between the

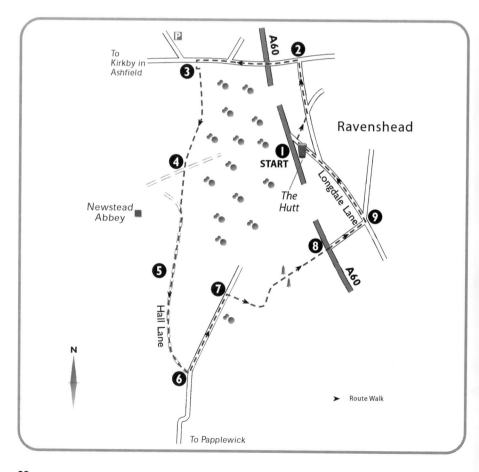

The view towards Newstead Abbey

wall on the left and various redbrick properties on the right. Keep forward to reach an open field on your right. Stay on the left side of this. The path then dips into a hollow at the end of the field – ignore the informal path to the right. Climb the steps and enter the woodland. This is full of oak and beech trees with a few silver birches thrown in for good measure. The paths forks at the point where ahead of you, at the bottom of a slope, you'll see a tarmac lane. Keep forward to the lane, ignoring the right fork.

❹ Cross this lane, which leads to Newstead Abbey, and rise up the path beyond. You subsequently join a single track tarmac lane and here you should bear left along it. A little way after this there is a seat on the right and a view of the Abbey. Relax awhile. The lane loses height and is then a steady straight walk for a while.

❺ Just before reaching a lodge, keep to the right of the driveway to pass through an old metal kissing gate. A lovely wide grassy path awaits you. Keep forward and continue on this as it becomes a gravel track. Nearly ³/₄ mile after passing the lodge keep forward passing Montagu Lodge to your right. The track bears left and you reach a grass triangle at the end of Hall Lane, which you have been walking along.

❻ Turn left along Blidworth Waye, crossing to the far side of the road where there is a narrow path beyond the ditch.

Some 60 yards later follow the Robin Hood Way as it enters the wood. This proceeds with the road to your left and is a much nicer and safer option than the road. Leave the wood and use the right hand verge beside the road for 70 or 80 yards. You then have the chance to walk through another narrow roadside wood until, again, you have to come out beside the road. Continue on the verge beyond for 130 yards or so.

7 On reaching the entrance to Newstead Grange on the left, turn right and walk away from the road for 500 yards beside a hedge on your right. In the bottom corner of the field turn left for 250 yards then bear right into the plantation. Keep on the same line to enter what looks like heathland. Continue

through this to reach a track at the top of a bank ahead of you. Turn left here before, 50 yards later, turning right to cross the track and walk up the right side of the wood ahead. Stay beside the fence on your right as it bears left then right to walk to the main road, the A60, ahead.

8 Cross the road carefully and walk along Kighill Lane for 500 yards.

9 Turn left into Longdale Lane for ³/₄ mile. Ignore all roads off to the right and subsequently some to the left. This brings you back to the Hutt.

Date walk completed:

....

Places of Interest Nearby

Newstead Abbey was the home of Lord Byron and the gardens are open all year round. With the parkland there's over 300 acres to explore. Telephone: 01623 455900.

The Hearty Goodfellow

A town and country walk that nearly, but not quite, completes the circuit of Southwell itself. The Southwell Trail proves a nice way of leaving the town to gain access to Norwood Park. On the way back the Robin Hood Way completes the circle giving good views of the Minster too. Now, whether it is pronounced Suthell or South-well, I'll leave to you to decide.

Distance: *5³/₄ miles*

OS Explorers 270 Sherwood Forest and 271 Newark on Trent
GR 702539

A few minor climbs shouldn't cause undue concern.

Starting point: The car park on Church Street opposite the Minster. Alternatively park in the car park of the Hearty Goodfellow, after gaining permission from the landlord, and turn right along Church Street until you reach Normanton Prebend where you turn right.

How to get there: Follow the A612 through Southwell.

There can't be many pubs called the **Hearty Goodfellow** but here's one. It is a nice pub with a very big beer garden beside a stream, which is very popular in summertime. There may even be a barbecue going when you get there. There is a good range of dishes, including pies, bangers, and grills plus excellent Everards, (Tiger, Tiger Chilled and Mild amongst others). There is even a website: www.theheartygoodfellow.co.uk.

Opening times are weekdays 12 noon to 3 pm and 6 pm to 11 pm. Saturday and Sunday they open 'all day'.

Telephone: 01636 812365.

85

The Walk

1 From the car park entrance, with the Minster ahead of you, turn left down Church Street and 175 yards later, immediately beyond Normanton Prebend, fork left off the road along the tarmac path. After a few yards, fork right, along a grassy path, walking beside a fence on your left. Stay beside the fence, negotiate a stile, before descending to and crossing a tarmac path, rising up the steps beyond into a field. Keep on the right side of the field beside a stream on your right. Ignore a footbridge to your right to reach the end of the field. With the stream still on your right you reach a road.

2 Cross the main road, following the tarmac path ahead, when 40 yards later you reach another road. Bear left along this with houses on your left and the stream on your right. The road bears right until you pass to the right of house number 18. With the stream still with you, you reach the main road.

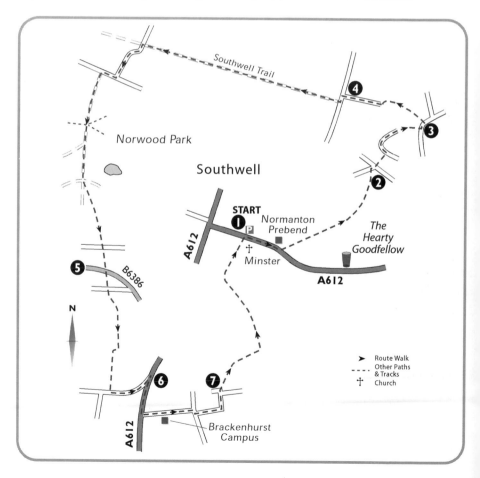

Norwood Park is seen from the route

❸ Turn left, and left again beyond The Gatehouse into a park, now with another stream on your right. Follow the path through this park, ignoring a number of paths to the left. Eventually you have to climb some steps to bring you up amongst the houses. Turn right here to reach another main road.

❹ Turn left, then almost immediately right along the Southwell Trail. Walk straight forward along this for nearly a mile to reach a lane. Turn left along this to reach a T-junction. Turn right for 100 yards then left along the driveway for Norwood Park. With the golf clubhouse to your right 350 yards later, ignore tracks to left and right and 100 yards later, at a grass triangle, again ignore the

right fork. Another 150 yards later, at a crossroads, take the path through the fruit trees ahead of you. Keep straight forward on this for a third of a mile to reach a lane. Cross this bearing slightly left uphill to reach the B6386 to the right of a red-brick house.

❺ Cross this, following the path opposite. This leads to another road. Turn right for a few yards then left between hedges to reach a bridge. Proceed along the left side of the field beyond. Cross a larger footbridge, climbing up the steps beyond into another field. Keep straight forward and, ignoring a path to left and right at the top of the steps, bear just slightly right to rise up to the end of the hedge ahead of you.

At the hedge corner go straight forward, keeping the hedge on your left. Keep on the left side of the next field. In the bottom left corner of the field, cross a bridge and turn right along the Robin Hood Way. Some 60 yards later turn left within the same field to walk up beside the hedge on your right. Continue on the right side of the field beyond to reach a narrow tarmac lane. Turn left here to the A612.

6 Turn right up the A612 to reach Nottingham Trent University's Brackenhurst Campus. Ignore the first left turn into the college but take the second one to walk through the college buildings. A quarter of a mile later, keep forward at a crossroads. The lane you're on then does a left turn.

7 Beyond Park Hill, 150 yards later ignore a lane to the right, keeping straight forward to pass through a gateway into a field. From here walk half right across the field along the Robin Hood Way again. Some 300 yards later bear slightly right across a second field. At the far side of the field, turn left within the field, to walk towards Southwell beside a hedge on your right. In the bottom right corner of the field keep on between fences. Turn right at a tarmac path, then left over a stream 25 yards later. Follow the drive up the right side of the War Memorial Recreation Ground. At the top beside an archway, turn right and continue forward into the Minster grounds. From here you should be able to find your way back to your car.

Date walk completed:

....

Places of Interest Nearby

The most obvious place to visit is 12th century **Southwell Minster**. It is an absolutely stunning building. Telephone: 01636 812649. Then there's the **National Trust Workshouse** which you pass on the walk. Telephone: 01636 817250.

Awsworth 25
The Gardeners Inn

This is D.H. Lawrence country, and hemmed in as it is by Nottingham, Eastwood and Ilkeston, it is hard to imagine there being much countryside worth exploring. Get a load of this though: the Nottingham Canal, a memorial to the dead of Waterloo, crossing the M1, as well as passing under it, a lovely small Woodland Trust wood and there's Strelley, and much more.

The **Gardeners Inn** is a fairly new pub with a good choice of food and Hardys and Hansons beer. You won't go hungry here with hot snacks, jacket potatoes and ploughman's lunches on offer as well as more substantial fare such as Gardeners Mixed Grill, Cumberland sausage and beef in red wine.

Distance: *7 miles*

OS Explorer 260 Nottingham GR 482436

No real ascents to worry about.

Starting point: The Gardeners Inn, but be sure to ask the landlord first before leaving your car whilst walking.

How to get there: From the A610 follow the A6096 south. At the first roundabout bear left through Awsworth. The inn is on the left about half a mile later.

Opening times: Food is served during the week from 12 noon to 2 pm and 6 pm to 8 pm and at the weekend from 12 noon to 2 pm.

Telephone: 0115 9323087.

The Walk

❶ From the entrance of the Gardeners Inn car park turn right to the crossroads just a few yards away. Turn left along Newtons Lane. Keep forward at the end of the houses. Away to your right is an impressive viaduct. Cross the A6096 continuing along Newtons Lane opposite. On the far side of the canal turn left alongside it.

❷ On reaching the A6096 again, cross this by the pelican, noting the bridleway crossing too! Ignore all paths to the left for the next ³⁄₄ mile. As you proceed the path crosses over a road before descending and then ascending back to the level of the canal. Turn left uphill on the wide gravel bridleway that crosses the canal. Stay on this to reach a road corner. Turn left uphill towards Cossall church with its Waterloo monument. Swing left along the road past Church Cottage with its connections with D.H. Lawrence and then pass Willoughby Almshouses on your right. On the right hand bend, immediately beyond Rose Cottage, 150 yards later, turn left along the fenced path across the field. This brings you back to the bridleway you were on earlier. Follow the path opposite down the right side of the field to reach the canal again.

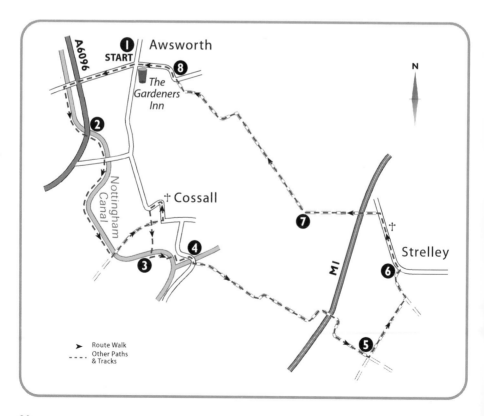

The Waterloo monument in the churchyard at Cossall

❸ Turn left on the far side of the canal. Cross the first footbridge after 250 yards and bear right with the canal now on your right. Follow the path round to the left alongside Robbinetts Arm, as the spur off the canal is known. There is quite often a heron around here so look out for it.

❹ At the road turn right for a few yards before crossing it carefully. Take the bridleroad for Trowell and Balloon House. After about 200 yards, ignore a path to the right. Stay on the obvious hedged bridle road until through a gap you'll see the M1 ahead. Continue towards the motorway until with it almost straight in front of you the bridleroad swings left before passing under the M1. On the far side of the M1 swing right parallel to it for 120 yards before bearing left for 450 yards.

❺ This brings you to a crossroads of bridleroads. Turn left here for Strelley and Kimberley. Walk up the right side of Shaw's Plantation. Away to the right is Nottingham and prominent in Wollaton Park is Wollaton Hall. Keep on the bridleroad for 600 yards beyond the plantation. On reaching a T-junction of bridleways turn left keeping a hedge beside you on your right. This bridleway swings right after 400 yards to bring you to a road.

❻ Turn left along this towards All Saints Church, Strelley. Two hundred yards later with the entrance to Strelley Hall on your right, turn left and follow the bridleway, a wide farm track which takes you *over* the M1 this time around. Beyond the motorway ignore a footpath on your right after about 100 yards but feel free to enter Holly Copse, a Woodland Trust property, just a few yards later. This is a delightful small wood beside the bridleway and as long as you get back on the bridleway you'll be okay!

❼ At the end of the wood, stay on the bridleway as it keeps forward between a pair of driveways. Similarly keep forward 300 yards later with a drive either side of the bridleway again. This bridleway leads you directly towards Strelley Park Farm, a rather grand place, though just in front of it take the bridleway on the left for Cossall and Awsworth. It is only supposition but there is a good chance that D.H. Lawrence will have walked this way. It is only two or three miles from where he grew up at Eastwood and he knew the countryside hereabouts very well. Ignore the footpath to Cossall village on the left as you enjoy this delightful hedged bridleway. Stay on the bridleway where it swings right for Cossall and Awsworth, ignoring a footpath along a grassy track to the left.

❽ On reaching a bend in the road, walk straight forward, ignoring the road to the right. Some 100 yards later the road bends left. Follow this into Awsworth with the Gardeners Inn on the left.

Date walk completed:
....

Places of Interest Nearby
You're in D.H.Lawrence country so why not visit **D.H.Lawrence Heritage** at Eastwood. Follow the signs from the A610. There are two sites, **Lawrence's Birthplace Museum** and **Durban House Heritage Centre**. Telephone: 01773 717353.

Cornmill at Chilwell

This easy walk on the outskirts of Nottingham is likely to be a real revelation to those who don't know the area. It really is an eye-opener as you pass the village of Attenborough and wander through the paths in the Nature Reserve with so many wildfowl. Take your binoculars because there is always something to be seen either in the Nature Reserve or on the River Trent.

The Cornmill is a busy Hardys and Hansons pub with a wide choice of food. There is something for everyone with standards like rump steak and liver and onions or you can have something more unusual like mushroom xacuti! The beers are all Hardys and Hansons including Olde Trip and Best Bitter with guests such as Guzzling Goose.

Opening times Food is available every day from 11 am to 10 pm except Sunday when it is 12 noon until 9 pm.

Telephone: 0115 9462913.

Distance: *3³/₄ miles*

OS Explorer 260 Nottingham
GR 516339

Probably the flattest walk you could wish for.

Starting point: The Attenborough Nature Reserve

How to get there: Follow the A6005 east from Long Eaton. Look out for Attenborough Nature Reserve Signs. Follow these until you reach the Reserve's car park. Assuming you follow the A6005 from Long Eaton, The Cornmill pub is at the crossroads where you turn right to the Nature Reserve.

The Walk

❶ From the car park walk north-eastwards towards the church spire in Attenborough. This path soon runs between two ponds. When the path splits, fork left along the bridleway for Attenborough village and church. Keep forward passing the church on your right.

❷ On reaching the corner of a road turn right towards the church gates. Follow the road round to the left and stay on it.

❸ In 100 yards, at a T-junction, turn right before bearing left round the corner, signed 'Meadow Lane, Attenborough'

ignoring a footpath to your right. Keep forward at the 'No through road' sign. After passing various houses you're back in the countryside, walking beside a pond to your left. Cross a footbridge over a working waterway. Shortly afterwards keep straight forward with the pond still on your left. Again, shortly beyond this, keep forward for Meadow Lane, ignoring another path to your right. You should now be in the trees with the ponds behind you.

❹ The path bears slightly right beside the railway line to London before you turn right for the River Trent and Beeston Marina. This reserve is managed by

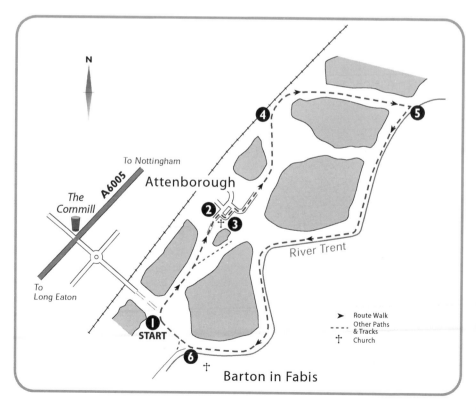

94

An enchanting view of Attenborough and the church of St Mary

Nottinghamshire Wildlife Trust and Broxtowe Borough Council, having been used originally for sand and gravel extraction. Once again the path runs between ponds.

5 About 600 yards from the railway line you reach the River Trent. Beeston Marina is to your left whilst Trent Lock is to your right. Turn right and stay beside the Trent for 1^1/$_2$ miles ignoring all paths to the right. As you get towards the end of this distance, on a fairly tight right-hand bend in the river, the buildings of Barton in Fabis are clearly visible across the river.

The cooling towers of Ratcliffe on Soar Power Station are beyond Barton.

6 With Barton in Fabis across the river to your left, the path forks. Take the right fork for 30 yards or so. Then take the right turn, ignoring a footbridge to your left, for Barton Lane car park. Leaving the Trent behind you continue along the gravel track back to the car.

Date walk completed:

....

Places of Interest Nearby

Choose between the new centre at **Attenborough Nature Reserve**, telephone: 0115 9170416; or **Wollaton Hall and Park** which you will have glimpsed from the route of the walk, telephone: 0115 9153900. You will have some idea what is at the Nature Reserve but as regards Wollaton, it is a 500-acre park with a natural history museum, gallery, gardens and lakes.

27 *Colston Bassett*
The Martins Arms

From the lovely village of Colston Bassett with its marvellous country store you walk alongside the disused Grantham Canal to reach Cropwell Bishop. A bridleway leads you to the ruined church of St Mary's which you may want to explore before you cross the fields back into Colston Bassett and a well earned lunch stop.

Distance: 5³⁄₄ miles

OS Explorer 260 Nottingham
GR 699332

A level undemanding walk.

Starting point: The Martins Arms. Park in the pub car park, with the landlord's permission, or the road nearby.

How to get there: Colston Bassett is to the south-east of Nottingham, south of the A52 between Langar and Kinoulton.

The **Martins Arms** is the archetypal English pub, full of character, with good beer, excellent food and very friendly helpful staff. It is an excellent pub. It may cost a little more than one or two other pubs but you get real quality food here. Be sure to sample the banana bread and butter pudding if it's on offer, it's absolutely delectable. Before that though you would probably want to try dishes like braised lamb shank, potato cake and crackling cod.

Opening times on weekdays and Saturday, from 12 noon until 3 pm and 6 pm until 11 pm. On Sunday, from 12 noon until 3 pm and then 6.30 pm until 10.30 pm. Food is available every day from 12 noon until 2 pm and from 6 pm until 10 pm (except Sunday evening).

Telephone: 01949 81361.

The Walk

1 From the pub car park turn right along the lane away from the church. Pass a number of properties. Immediately beyond The Cottage, the last house on the right, cross the stile on the right. Follow a vague grassy track towards some double gates 350 yards away across the field. Pass through both sets of gates. From here, head towards the gate in front, 180 yards away. Then walk along the track beyond to reach a lane.

2 Turn left along the lane for just over ¹/₂ mile.

3 On reaching Spencer's Bridge (No. 24) which takes the road over the disused Grantham Canal, turn right to walk along the towpath of the canal. Stay on this for about a mile.

4 On approaching another lane bear right up to it before turning left to pick up the canal on the far side – ignore the public footpath here. The bridge here is

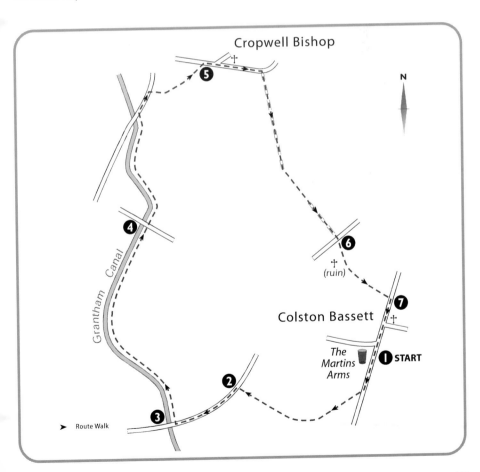

*The ruined church of St Mary at
Colston Bassett*

No. 23. Continue beside the canal to pass
The Old Mill to reach the road beyond.
Proceed along the road as it bends left.
Just before the road straightens out, turn
right into the field to walk away from the
road with a hedge on your left. After 120
yards cross a stile on the left and walk
diagonally right, across the field towards
a pair of electricity poles. Then in the
third field bear slightly left aiming for the
gable end of the building nearest to you.
Walk along the gravel path then a
driveway to come out at the entrance to
Richard's Close in Cropwell Bishop.

5 Turn right along the road. Pass the
church on your left. Stay on the main
road. Pass the Manor on your right.
Beyond this turn right along a bridleway
[Pasture Lane] passing Manor Farm. Half
a mile later, where the track ends, bear

half left across the field to a bridlegate.
Beyond this, walk along the left side of
the field beside a hedge on your left.
Continue forward passing the orchard of
Home Farm on your left. Pass through a
gateway just beyond the farmhouse to
reach a driveway. Bear right along this
with a wood on your right. This brings
you to a lane.

6 Cross the lane. Ahead is the ruin of St
Mary's church. Take the chance to have a
look round. Return to the bridleway
continuing in the same direction as
before, descending into a shallow valley.
Cross the concrete bridge and follow the
bridleway. This swings round to pass
behind a cricket pavilion. Ignore a path
to your right just before the pavilion.
Beyond the pavilion proceed alongside a
hedge on your left and keep forward. A
substantial bridge takes you over a quiet
stream and you should continue to a lane.

7 Turn right along this passing the
church on your left. As the road swings
round to the right in front of the Martins
Arms get on the left side of the road to
return to the pub.

Date walk completed:

....

Place of Interest Nearby
Six miles or so due east of Colston Bassett stands **Belvoir Castle** in Leicestershire, the ancestral
home of the Dukes of Rutland. For further information, telephone 01476 871000.

pursued to its tidal limit at Surfleet Seas End, returning via a winding riverbank footpath. There is much to see at Surfleet Seas End where a huge sluice gate divides two starkly contrasting landscapes. The Macmillan Way and the Brown Fen Waterway Trail are followed for much of the way, and a halt at a popular waterside inn is the treat to spur you on your way.

Here is a very simple fenland walk, but intriguing nevertheless. From Surfleet's tilting church spire (Pisa's tower leans less!) the River Glen is

Distance: *4 miles*

OS Explorer 249 (Spalding and Holbeach) or Landranger 131 (Boston and Spalding). GR 251281

This walk, level throughout, is equally divided between firm road walking and good grass riverbank paths.

Starting point: The Mermaid at the bridge over the River Glen in Surfleet. The best place to park is along Station Road near the start of the walk.

How to get there: Surfleet is situated 4 miles north of Spalding and can be reached either by following the B1356 from Spalding town centre or by turning off the A16 onto the A152 then turning left onto the B1356 at the next roundabout.

The Mermaid's setting on the banks of the River Glen is so splendid they've even built an outdoor bar in the gardens. With a long-established reputation for fine food this grand brick-built inn remains unspoilt inside, although a large restaurant has been added to the original lounge and dining area. The mouthwatering menu includes such favourites as steak and ale pie 'Mermaid style' as well as a number of dishes served with tempting sauces – the duck in Black Forest fruits sauce is just one. On Sunday lunchtimes all menus are replaced by a choice of roast lunches, while the line up on the bar includes Adnam's Broadside, John Smith's Cask and Tetley's Smoothflow.

Opening times are from 11.30 am to 11 pm daily, (Sunday from 12 noon) and meals are served from 12 noon to 2 pm and from 6.30 pm to 9 pm every day.

Telephone: 01775 680275

The Walk

1 Cross the main road from the Mermaid and proceed along Station Road, having first visited the extraordinary leaning spire of Saint Laurence's church – 'like a ship lurching at sea' according to Mee. In fact the tower began to tilt almost as soon as it was completed and the tip of its spire is now 6 ft 4¹/₂ ins from the vertical. Also of note are the rebuilt rood loft and a stone effigy of Sir Hugh Cressy, who died in 1347. The River Glen quickly comes alongside Station Road and begins a tenuous relationship with your route, which it will desert and rejoin several times. After a mile, branch right at a shop and post office into an unnamed road, which terminates abruptly at the Riverside Hotel. The busy road barring your way follows the former course of the railway from Boston to Spalding, but all traces of both station and level crossing have vanished.

2 Cross the A16 by means of the ramps and the tunnel and continue along the lane, on the far side. Pass a low thatch and a converted chapel before you turn right, into a lane signposted for Surfleet Seas End. Half a mile along this lane the furthest extent of the walk is reached at the Ship, a restored inn bearing a colossal painting of a sailing vessel on one side. But there is much to explore before the return journey, and by ascending the levee here you will be confronted by the confluence of three major waterways, the rivers Welland and Glen and the man-made Vernatt's Drain.

3 Follow the banktop to the right as far as a huge sluice gate, built in 1879 to replace an earlier sluice of 1739. The level of the river inland from here is

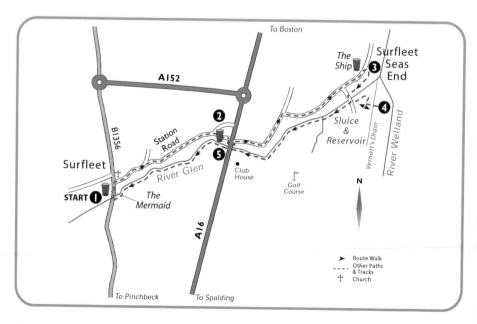

The River Glen at Surfleet Seas End

maintained for constant navigability and is known confusingly as the 'Reservoir'. Here an idyllic holiday retreat has developed. Chalets sit back from the neat lawns of the riverbanks, pleasure craft ply back and forth in summer and children can even be seen splashing in and out of the water. But on the tidal side of the sluice the ebb and flow of the muddy waters have formed quite a different picture. Rotting timber hulls lying in the muddy creeks and rows of crooked wooden jetties rising from the endless reed beds strike a quite surreal image. Contrast the two. Two information boards at the sluice explain the area's history, especially of the ceaseless battle to prevent the sea from reclaiming these fertile fens. To best view this marshy watersmeet follow the track on the bank leading from these boards in a wide curve until it reaches the bridge over Vernatt's Drain. Along here are the best spots to inspect the boats below you.

4 Continue over the bridge as far as the banks of the impassable Welland before returning to the sluice. Now strike out along the grassy riverbank past the chalets with the Glen on your right. At the last chalet, climb to a concrete track, which you follow as far as a wide bridge and a gate on the right. On the other side of the gate is a private golf course and the right of way, manicured to the same standard as the rest of the links, hugs the riverbank faithfully. Near to the clubhouse a short fenced section takes you back to the busy A16 and the same manoeuvre is repeated – steps, tunnel, steps again.

5 On the far side, the banktop footpath now continues along the edge of an arable field, narrow and exposed. On the far bank can be seen the private landing stages and boats of the properties passed on the outward journey. Nearing Surfleet once more pass through a gap in the hedgerow where a number of willows drape over the surface of the river. You now find yourself in a surprising parkland of trimmed lawns and huge specimen trees. Follow the River Glen for one last stretch before your footpath passes below a new house and returns you to the road in Surfleet with the Mermaid opposite.

Date walk completed:

Place of Interest Nearby
Ayscoughee Hall in Spalding is a handsome medieval wool merchant's home converted to house a number of exhibitions and attractions, including a comprehensive Land Drainage Gallery. The Pavilion Café and ancient Yew Walks can be found in the 5 acres of walled gardens. Telephone 01775 725468 for details.

The Black Horse

walk is a magical trip leading you far from the bustle of everyday life and linking a series of villages built entirely of stone. You will twice pass through the parkland of Grimsthorpe Castle, often densely wooded and criss-crossed by 'Ridings'. Sensational views of the castle are a highlight, and attractive stretches of the East and West Glen Rivers are taken in. You may even be fortunate enough to spot a herd of deer from the estate.

This is one of only a few walks where the starting point requires a short drive from the pub. The

Distance: *8 miles*

OS Explorer248 (Bourne and Heckington) or Landranger 130 (Grantham) GR of pub 047230

A challenging walk involving some steep hills. Several sections can be muddy.

Starting point: The walk begins at St Michael's church in Edenham. You will be able to park in the streets around the church.

How to get there: From Bourne, head west along the A151 towards Grantham. In 3 miles you will reach the start of the walk in Edenham, and the Black Horse in Grimsthorpe is just a mile further on.

It is easy to miss the **Black Horse**, when admiring the stately outline of the castle as you pass through Grimsthorpe. This splendid old stone inn sits proudly behind its gravel courtyard framed by tall trees and rows of stables. The meals on offer in the Pheasantry are all of extremely high quality and exquisitely presented. The Rutland sausages and steak, ale and mushroom pie are popular, as are the roasts added to the menu at lunchtime on Sundays. As well as the expected beers and lagers three guest ales, selected only from small local breweries, are always available.

Opening times are from 12 noon to 2 pm every day and from 6 pm to 11 pm (Sunday 7 pm to 10 pm). Food is served from 12 noon to 2 pm and 6 pm to 9 pm (No meals available on Sunday evening).

Telephone: 01778 591247.

The Walk

❶ Turn left from the church, crossing the East Glen River and then right, into Scottlethorpe Road. A mile and a half along this dwindling lane, now deep into tranquil wooded parkscape, do not follow the metalled surface at a sharp turn to the left towards Scottlethorpe Grange but continue straight ahead on a chalky track heading through the woods.

❷ Just 400 yards along here a signed footpath on your right takes you onto a short open path between fields and into the parkland belonging to Grimsthorpe Castle. Turn right and follow the perimeter of the wood in front of you as far as a mighty wooden gate – Pebble Gate. Ahead of you now is a wide grassy avenue – this is Steel's Riding. Simply pursue this delightful trail for a full mile, negotiating a couple of stiles along the way. Between borders of bracken and briar and surrounded by ancient oaks, many in an advanced state of decay, it is a slightly eerie scene and particularly theatrical in winter.

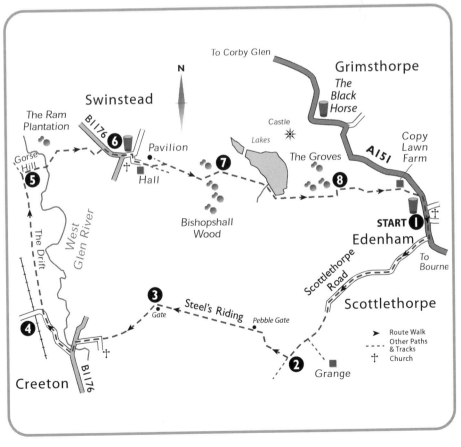

Grimsthorpe Castle seen from the road

❸ Leave the park via another handsome wooden gate and, after a series of narrower paths along the edges of four arable fields, you clear the next stile to find yourself on a lane above the tiny stone village of Creeton. Before descending into Creeton wander along the lane as far as the small but perfectly formed stone broach spire of Saint Peter's church. Returning, turn left when you reach the main B1176 in Creeton then branch right at the turning signed for Counthorpe.

❹ In half a mile the road swings left to pass beneath the GNER route linking London with the north of England. Your route, however, continues straight ahead on a grassy (and sometimes muddy) track

known as the Drift. This exciting switchback is littered in parts with colossal limestone boulders, presumably debris from the nearby quarry at Counthorpe. The views across the deep wide valley of the West Glen River are stunning and tell of a prehistoric age when the Glen must have been a powerful glacial force indeed.

❺ Turn right and follow a footpath sign indicating a lesser track leading down Gorse Hill on your right. Cross the footbridge over the West Glen River at the foot of the valley and ascend the grassy bank on the far side, picking a way between the bright gorse bushes and keeping as your target the right hand edge of the wood on the skyline ahead of you. The view back over the valley of the lazy meandering Glen gradually eroding its own banks should not be missed. Clearing a stile in the very corner of the field your path now follows a hedge past two fields of crop to a gated farm track onto which you turn left. Turn right when you reach the road to enter the stone-built village of Swinstead.

❻ Continue past the cross and the church and turn right into Park Road at a pub named the Windmill. Follow Park Road as it swings to the left and remain on it until you spot a track shooting off left towards the hidden Summer House, an impressive stone pavilion erected in the 1720s by Sir John Vanbrugh, who so spectacularly remodelled the façade of Grimsthorpe Castle. At this point a clear footpath slants diagonally across the narrow field on your left towards a plantation, where it joins a better track heading towards the towering trees of Bishopshall Wood. As you emerge from this wood you are arrested by the sight of Grimsthorpe Castle on the skyline, breathtakingly viewed over the lake and framed by its surrounding park and woodland.

❼ Select the grassy track leading half-right down the hillside towards the lake,

then follow the edge of the water over a footbridge and onto a metalled surface which passes a distinctive group of old oak trees. When you see an open track leaving the tarmac on the right follow this for just a few yards, turn left at a haystack towards a gate and ascend the steep track leading up the hillside to reluctantly exit these dramatic surroundings and enter a belt of woodland. Follow the clear track through the woods and back into the sunlight before rounding the corner of the wood, now on a narrower field path.

❽ A few yards past this corner your footpath branches right, to follow a ditch and, past a stile and a footbridge, continues over two meadows and through two more gates, finally arriving at a farmyard. Once in the yard, however, do not follow the muddy track but seek a high stile on your right, the first of three that guide you over two more pastures and back onto the road in Edenham. The church and your starting point are now just a short walk to your right.

Date walk completed:

Walk 30 *South Witham*
The Blue Cow

western boundary of the county. A series of brooks hasten through these undulating fields to swell the youthful Witham on its long journey to Lincoln and Boston. A link with an even more historic era is found in the fields where once stood one of the Knights Templar's most important preceptories. The first class Blue Cow Inn and Brewery conforms to the local pattern – the powerful Tollemarches political persuasions once dictated that all inns hereabouts should bear the title 'Blue'.

Four fascinating villages built almost entirely of old stone punctuate this peaceful rural walk along the

Distance: *6 miles*

OS Explorer 247 (Grantham) or Landranger 130 (Grantham). GR 927192

This is a challenging walk, involving a variety of terrain, including some field paths.

Starting point: The Blue Cow in South Witham. The best place to park is on the roadside near to the village shop in Water Lane.

How to get there: South Witham is situated just a mile west of the A1, 3 miles south of Colsterworth. The turn-off is clearly signed and leads straight to the Blue Cow in the village.

What makes the **Blue Cow** unique is neither its setting in this attractive stone village, the worn flagstones and low beams inside the welcoming building nor the high quality of the food on offer. It is the fact that the only beers served are brewed on the premises in the award-winning micro-brewery beneath the pub. Thirlwell's Best Bitter and Witham Wobbler both come highly recommended, as do all meals on the menu, which changes on a weekly basis. If the generous main course portions daunt you, a choice of baguettes and warm 'American' sandwiches are available, while vegetarians and children are also well catered for.

Opening times are 12 noon to 11 pm (Sunday to 10.30 pm). Meals are available every day between 12 noon and 2.30 pm and again between 6 pm and 9.30 pm.

Telephone: 01572 768432

106

The Walk

1 Set off left from the Blue Cow and promptly turn right into Water Lane to pass the village shop. Along here a clearly signed footpath on the left leads you around the village hall and diagonally across a playing field to unite with the infant River Witham, here a mere brook. Just into the next field a footbridge crosses the river and takes you into an area of modern housing. Follow Templar's Way to the left, around the corner and up the hill. Look for a footpath sign by a pair of garages on the left and, passing through the gap in the hedge here, continue along the field's edge to a lane at the top of the hill.

2 Cross Moor Lane, vault a stile and pursue the clear path in the same direction through the crop in the field ahead. Now in pleasant open countryside keep the church spire in far-off Stainby as your goal through the next series of fields. Over a footbridge at the end of the first field follow the short winding track to the left before locating the path

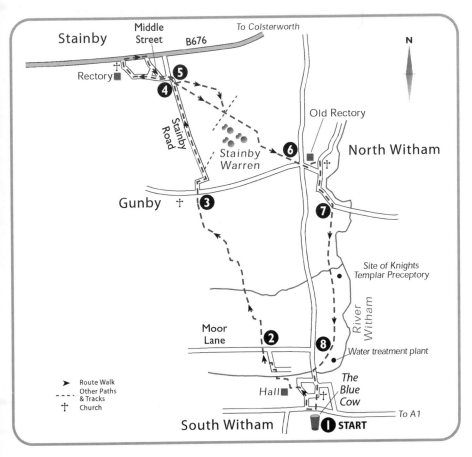

107

River Witham at North Witham

heading across the next field. Now look first for a yellow post then a lone sycamore at a bridge over a tiny tributary of the Witham, one of several encountered on the journey. Follow the hedge to the next boundary then slant half-left across another field targeting the wooden rail of a footbridge set in the hedge ahead. Part-way into the next field another brook bars your way – follow this left to a corner from where a clear field-edge path continues north to meet the valley road in the farming hamlet of Gunby.

❸ To your left here is a stunning setting. The grassy banks of Gunby's gurgling stream slope upwards to stone manors, houses and farm buildings, and the small church at the top of the hill is the best

spot from which to survey this scene. Climb out of Gunby by the lane signed for Stainby, noting the words 'Blue Fox' neatly picked out above the door of the former inn. Continue along this quiet elevated lane for almost a mile until it bridges another stream.

❹ Turn left here to enter Water Lane in Stainby, another village of immaculate stone houses congregating in the trees alongside the crystal-clear stream. Naturally enough, Water Lane adheres to the stream until it suddenly rears up the hillside towards another imposing group of stone buildings, the sturdy walls surrounding the Old Rectory and the adjacent church. Turn right at the church and follow the main road, the B676, past a horse paddock. Turn right again into

Middle Street which sweeps obliquely down the hillside to rejoin Water Lane and return you to the bridge. Set off back in the direction of Gunby but turn into the first track on your left.

5 A hidden but signed stile in the hedge at this point indicates the true right of way – over three fields of crop via two clear footbridges to reach another stile. If these paths are not in place the stile can be reached by following the track round in a rough semicircle. Both routes aim for the corner of a large wood (Stainby Warren), to the left of which the path continues in its original direction across the adjacent field. Through the gap in the hedge ahead, plunge straight down the hillside to cross a wooden footbridge. Your route now climbs through the next three fields, once more in a diagonal direction. Again, if the paths are not in place, make use of the field boundaries. In either case you are aiming for the conspicuous white corrugated hut at the crossroads above North Witham.

6 Reaching this junction head immediately down Rectory Lane towards the village. At the Old Rectory seek a signed footpath on the left which cuts behind the houses to emerge on a tiny lane at the church – the recessed spire can be seen between two rows of neatly trimmed yews. Now turn south along Church Street and continue out of the village accompanied by the delightful bubbling waters of the Witham.

7 After following the river around the wide bend, branch onto the first signed footpath on your right, struggle to the top of the hill before losing all the height just gained and rejoining the river coming in from your left. The path through the next series of fields is intermittent, but where it is indistinct simply keep the river to your left and navigational errors cannot occur. What you do need to know is that the third of the six fields is the site of the 12th century Preceptory of the Knight's Templar. This was one of the Templars' wealthiest estates, and several features can still be identified amongst the mounds and hollows.

8 Eventually hurdling a stile above a water treatment plant a final path slants across a pasture to rejoin the road in South Witham. From here the way back to the Blue Cow is straight on, ignoring all turnings and obstacles. Pass the Angel on Church Lane and the tiny church, crowned by its two-bell turret, before a constricted passage guides you along the final yards to your starting point.

Date walk completed:

....

Places of Interest Nearby
Woolsthorpe Manor, three miles to the north is the 17th century farmhouse made famous as the home of Sir Isaac Newton. As well as the new **Science Discovery Centre** you can even sit under a descendent of the apple tree that inspired the theory of gravity! Telephone 01476 860338.

The Houblon Inn

In the gently rolling hills to the west of Sleaford lie countless hidden hamlets of limestone houses and cottages. This ramble links four of these hamlets, and a

Distance: 4 miles

OS Explorer 248 (Bourne and Heckington) or Landranger 130 (Grantham) GR 004391

None of the gradients on this walk are challenging but the surface varies from good roads to muddy tracks and fields.

Starting point: The Houblon Arms in Oasby. Ask the landlord for permission to leave your vehicle, or park on the wider road passing through the village on its way from Culverthorpe to Welby.

How to get there: Oasby is situated approximately midway between Grantham and Sleaford. From Grantham head east along the A52, turn left in 6 miles then right after another mile. From Sleaford drive 3 miles south along the A15, take either of two signed roads to Swarby then bear right to pass through Culverthorpe and reach the village of Oasby. Either of the two lanes into the village leads you to the Inn.

chateau-style hall overlooking its lake adds grandeur to the outing. The earthworks of a former castle betray the one-time prominence of one of these hamlets, but the real highlight is a gem of a traditional country inn, popular despite its hidden location and restored to a very high standard.

The Houblon Inn, named after the local nobility and prominently displaying their coat of arms, has been recently restored to its former splendour. Roses climb the low limestone walls and colourful baskets hang by the shuttered windows, while inside huge flagstones, low beams and the smell of log fires conjure an even more elevated ambience. The meals live up to the surroundings and are so popular that larger groups and Sunday lunches should be booked prior to your visit – this is one treat you will not want to miss out on. The menu changes daily according to availability and season and might include chicken in a leek and Stilton sauce or autumn fruit crumble for dessert. Smaller portions are available for smaller mouths and the friendly staff are happy to accommodate most tastes and requirements. The Houblon is a free house and supports local breweries by rotating a number of guest beers, in addition to the regular Everard's Tiger.

Opening times are 12 noon to 2 pm (Sunday to 2.30 pm) and 6.30 pm to 11 pm (Sunday 7 pm to 10.30 pm). Meals are available between 12 noon and 2 pm and again between 6.30 pm and 9.30 pm. The Inn does not serve food on Sunday evenings and remains closed all day on Mondays.

Telephone: 01529 455215.

The Walk

1 Step from the door of the Houblon Inn and walk left between the rows of attractive stone houses. Reaching a t-junction turn left again and join the wider road. Shortly you will spot a footpath sign on your right – the grass path here is a short-cut past a playing field to a lane above the tiny hamlet of Aisby. Now follow the lane to the right admiring more fine stone buildings bordering Aisby's Millennium Green before continuing around the edge of the sloping Green to re-ascend the hill.

2 Just past the last farm building on the right seek a gap in the hedge from where a signed footpath slants across a field used for horse jumping to re-emerge on another lane via a footbridge. Turn right onto this hedge-lined lane and, after a

winding ½ mile, turn left onto a signed bridleway.

3 This track, often heavy underfoot, nevertheless offers superb views to Culverthorpe Hall and of the spires of Sleaford and its neighbouring villages dotted along the fenland skyline. Arriving at Culverthorpe Hollow turn right onto the road which climbs to a junction where an old cast iron signpost points mistakenly to the 'Hall Only'. Along here grand wrought iron gates welcome you into the opulent surroundings of Culverthorpe Park.

4 This is a section not to be hurried as the driveway wends past the dramatic frontage of the Hall flanked by striking ranges of mellow stone outbuildings, a matchless composition. When you reach the estate farm your track passes through

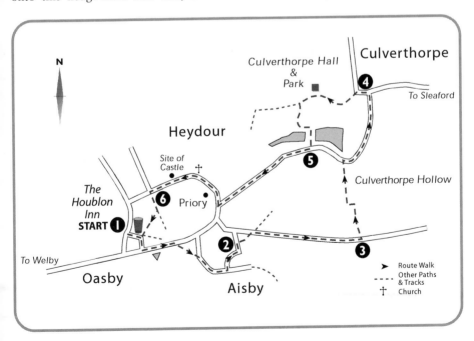

Culverthorpe Hall sits amongst opulent surroundings

two gates as it bends to the left. At this point a clear bridleway shoots off to the right across the fields to Heydour. The intrepid may choose this option – navigation is not difficult but access to the churchyard in Heydour can be confusing. Otherwise continue from the farm straight down the hill on the enclosed track, enjoying splendid views over the lakes before a causeway between the two bodies of water leads you back onto the road at a car park.

❺ Now turn right, along the road for fully half a mile before turning right again into Heydour when you see a clear road sign. More fascinating buildings accompany you through the leafy hamlet of Heydour. The Priory on your left was built in the 1500s and the church in the

hollow boasts a wealth of monuments to the Newtons from Culverthorpe Hall. The stone hall next to the church was once the rectory – a reclaimed 14th century statue of a musician with cymbals stands above the main door. Finally you pass a field on the right containing the earthworks of Heydour's former castle bailey before arriving at a signed footpath on your left which leads you clearly enough through a field of crop.

❻ Reaching a footbridge adjust your course by pivoting 45 degrees to the right to pursue the diagonal path across the next three meadows. Two easily identified stiles help you initially, but the exit stile from the third field is situated next to a chicken coop in the corner of the field. Now a short passageway guides you back to a shaded bench in Oasby, with the Houblon Inn just yards to your right.

Date walk completed:

....

Place of Interest Nearby
Six miles to the north-east the **Hub** in Sleaford is an exciting new centre for contemporary art and design. As well as regularly changing exhibitions and events displaying high quality crafts from around the world you will find an outstanding shop and café. Entrance is free - telephone 01529 308710 for details.

The width of the main road and the sheer number of elegant brick houses betray Long Bennington's one-time importance as a staging post on the Great North Road. Nowadays more tranquil, this is one of a triangle of villages visited, each possessing a similar church tower, all of which remain visible as landmarks for the entire journey. The lazy meandering Witham is twice crossed as it makes its way through this gentle countryside towards Lincoln.

On a route more commonly associated with large coaching inns the **Reindeer** is the village's least ostentatious pub, sitting at the back of its gravelled frontage behind colourful potted shrubs. Inside you cannot help but feel comfortable and relaxed amongst the cushions, the books and the clocks around the low-beamed lounge. In winter an old coal stove burns in the ingle, while in fine weather outdoor seating is provided to both front and rear. The quality of the meals is excellent and they are all exquisitely presented, freshly cooked and quite delicious. Guest beers such as Bombardier or Speckled Hen are regularly rotated on the bar next to John Smith's bitter and the usual lagers.

Distance: 4½ miles

OS Explorer 247 (Grantham) or Landranger 130 (Grantham). GR 836445

A fairly simple level walk

Starting point: The Reindeer in Long Bennington. You will have no difficulty parking along the main road.

How to get there: Long Bennington is situated just off the A1, equidistant from Newark and Grantham. Signed roads lead in from both directions and the Reindeer can be found on the main road through the village.

Opening times are 12 noon to 3 pm and 7pm to 11 pm (Sunday to 10.30 pm) Meals are available weekdays from 12 noon to 2 pm and from 7 pm to 9.30 pm (10 pm on Saturdays). However, although the pub is open as usual, no meals are available on Sundays.

Telephone: 01400 281382.

The Walk

❶ From the Reindeer head south along Long Bennington's broad Main Road, admiring the rows of fine brick buildings sitting back from the street. Turn left into Church Street, the first road on your left then ensure that you turn right almost immediately to remain on Church Street. As the surroundings become more rural the majestic pinnacled tower of Saint Swithin's church looms tall through the trees. Step briefly into the drive leading to the church lych-gate but then locate a stile hidden in the hedge on your right.

❷ Clearing the stile, follow the left-hand perimeter of a meadow until a footbridge takes you onto a track, now in open countryside. On the other side of the track you will see a ditch between two arable fields and your path follows the right-hand bank of the ditch as far as a small wood. Over another footbridge the path traces the edge of the wood before continuing along the hedgerow to a stile at a good road. Now follow this road left for fully half a mile, passing a fishing lake on your right before rising into the attractive village of Foston.

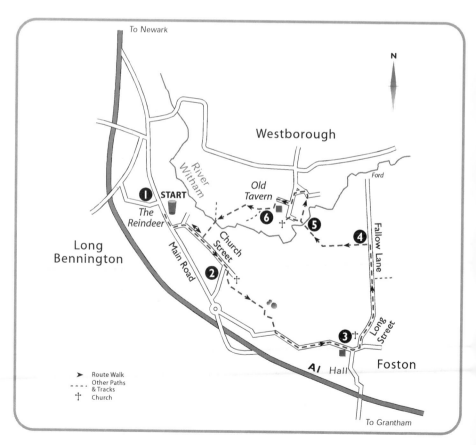

St Peter's church at Foston has a tractor weathervane

5 A railed footbridge takes you over the snaking Witham into Westborough. A thorough inspection of the beautiful interior of the church ahead should not be missed. Now backtrack towards the bridge for a few yards and seek a signed bridleway on the left leading you round the back of the village of Westborough to the shaded green at its centre. Having noted the stone steps of the old market cross (a more complete medieval cross exists in the churchyard) fork left towards the church once more. Turn right into Baker's Lane at the former 'Old Tavern' and follow this until a Viking Way sign directs you left onto a narrower hedge lined path.

3 At the three-way junction in the centre of the village admire the Old Hall, built of stone in 1647, before branching left into Long Street. Notice the weathervane atop the greystone tower of Saint Peter's church. It is in the form of a tractor, one of a series of unusual church vanes in Lincolnshire – Great Ponton has a violin, Partney a galleon. Long Street continues, out of the village as Fallow Lane, enjoying fine views over the shallow valley of the Witham to the villages on the Lincoln Cliff. The tower of Dry Doddington church, leaning precariously, is also visible.

6 Emerging into sunlight veer right across the next field to join another hedge which you proceed to follow in the same direction – do not be lured by a footpath shown on OS maps as a short-cut back to the river. Further along the hedgerow another clear Viking Way sign steers you half-left across the field to a gate near a clump of trees. Another clear path over the next meadow re-unites you with the wide River Witham, which you cross before ascending a short track to the road ahead. Realising that you are now back on Church Street in Long Bennington simply retrace your footsteps to the right, soon to arrive back at the Reindeer.

4 In less than a mile a clear bridleway sign ushers you left onto a short hedged track, at the end of which you continue across the next field of crop in the same direction. Two thirds of the way across this long field, however, the right of way suddenly veers half-right and makes a beeline for Westborough's church tower.

Date walk completed:

....

Place of Interest Nearby

Belton House is the perfect restoration country house to visit, just 7 miles from Long Bennington and 2 miles north of Grantham. Here you will also find extensive gardens, a shop, restaurant and adventure playground. Telephone: 01476 566116 for details of opening times and special events.

The walk from here links three interesting brick-built villages alongside the River Witham and through rolling arable fields to the south of Lincoln. One of the villages is littered with sculptures and mosaics and the second boasts the remains of a moated medieval site. Finally a stately 16th century hall set in immaculate grounds provides a suitable crescendo to the day's outing.

The **Royal Oak** has long been established as one of the county's most notable hostelries for food and drink. Bedecked with plants and flowers in all seasons, it looks every inch the traditional little village pub. Inside, however, the premises have been extended into a warren of dining areas large and small, and popular with locals and visitors. The menu is extensive, the portions generous and the freshly cooked food delicious. You will also find on offer several vegetarian options, a daily 'specials' sheet, a separate children's menu and a choice of less hearty snacks (the 'frisbees' are large filled circular rolls). A guest beer is always available alongside Adnam's Broadside, Timothy Taylor's Landlord and Bateman's XB.

Opening times are 12 noon to 2.30 pm Monday to Saturday; 7 pm to 11 pm Monday to Thursday; 6.30 pm to 11 pm Friday and Saturday; Sunday 12 noon to 10.30 pm. Meals can be ordered between 12 noon and 2 pm (3 pm on Sunday) and between 7 pm and 9 pm (6.30 pm on Friday and Saturday).

Telephone: 01522 788291.

Distance: *5 miles*

OS Explorer 272 (Lincoln) or Landranger 121 (Lincoln).
GR 925628

This is a mainly level walk.

Starting point: The Royal Oak in Aubourn. Park on the roadside around the one-way system or ask for permission to park at the pub.

How to get there: Head from Lincoln towards Newark on the A46. A mile south of the end of the by-pass a road signed for Aubourn leads off to the left to reach the village via Haddington. Alternatively turn off the A607 to Grantham at Harmston and Aubourn is 3 miles along this road.

The Walk

❶ Set off left along Royal Oak Lane, noticing at once one of the preserved Lion Head hydrants installed around the region in 1933. Turn right into Chapel Lane at the junction then branch immediately left into Moor Lane, indicated as a 'right of way to Bassingham'. Leaving Aubourn's handsome brick buildings behind, continue until Moor Lane downgrades to a track and leads you sharply to the right past a row of impressive oak trees.

❷ Swing left at the sign reading 'road used as a public path' and progress along the open track until it enters a narrower stretch enclosed by hedges to lead you as far as a firmer track. Turn right onto this track in the direction of the farm buildings then promptly branch left onto a path through the grass in the small field on the left. The footpath then makes its way along the right-hand edge of the narrow wood ahead to arrive at another firm track. Look carefully to your left at this point as two footpath signs guide you to a gap in the hedge through which a field edge path opens up. Continue straight across the field after this (or around the perimeter if no path is in place) to arrive at a road via a footbridge.

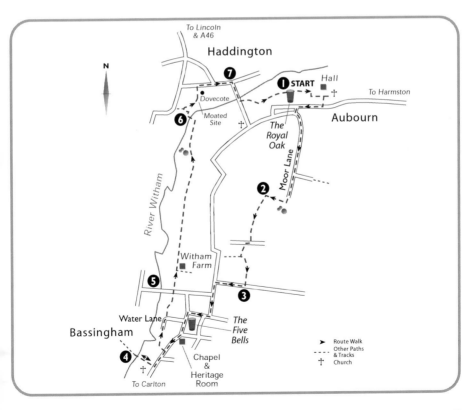

117

River Witham at Bassingham

❸ Follow the road to the right and turn left at the t-junction ahead to enter the substantial village of Bassingham. Remain on Lincoln Road as far as another t-junction, turn right along Linga Lane then left onto the High Street. There are many buildings of interest in Bassingham, in particular note the carved shutters on the striking red façade of the Five Bells inn. At a cluster of more imposing brick buildings stop to admire the Wesleyan Chapel of 1839. Now walk behind to the Heritage Room where a quite fascinating collection of local information has been assembled. The books and photographs here provide a valuable background to your tour of Bassingham and reflect great credit on the people of the village. It is well worth continuing through the village as far as the ornate church to inspect the bridge over the Witham at the end of the adjacent passageway.

❹ Now about turn and retrace your route into the High Street once more. Along here seek a hidden but signed footpath on the left just before a row of cottages. Follow this route carefully through the new housing to join Water Lane, and ensure that you do not miss another signed footpath on the left where this road bends. A stile by a stable now returns you to rural surroundings, and a kissing gate on the far side of the meadow leads you to a path along the hedgerow in the next field. This in turn takes you to Thurlby Road near to a bridge over the Witham.

5 On the far side of the road a short constricted stretch of track takes you to a footbridge, across a vegetable field and into a pasture via an aluminium gate. Pass below Witham Farm and continue to the kissing gate in the hedge ahead. Your path now heads straight across the next six fields of crop, finally aiming for the right-hand edge of a group of tall trees. A hidden footbridge here guides you onto one last field path, a colourful extravaganza of bright poppies and large daisies in season, to reach a railed concrete bridge over the foaming Witham.

6 Over the bridge to your left, turn right briefly and then into the lane that appears on your left. Further along the lane, stray into the field now on your right. The ridges and furrows around inform you that you have entered the medieval site of the moated Haddington Hall – a number of information boards explain the history of your surroundings. Make your way up to the square stone dovecote at the top of this site and exit via the gate, turning right onto Dovecote Lane. At the picturesque green in Haddington branch right into Butts Lane, having inspected the suspended bronze sculptures beneath the tree.

7 Turn right into Bridge Road where you spot a sign for Aubourn and head towards the spire of the crumbling Victorian church. Once over the river hurdle the stile on your left and head across the pasture, targeting the gap between the tall hedges ahead of you. Beyond the gap the path runs behind the gardens in Aubourn for some distance, encountering two more stiles on the way. When your progress is barred by the stunning lawns and gardens of Aubourn Hall a short track on your right leads you to a closed gate. Here another stile on your left allows you to enter and enjoy the Hall gardens at close quarters but do not stray from the conifer hedge. The Hall itself can be fully appreciated when you come to the main drive, and this wonderful section reaches a climax as you continue between the staddle stones as far as the tiny single nave of Saint Peter's church. Now leave this captivating setting, turn left onto the main drive and exit the grounds of the Hall at the impressive wooden gates. Your starting point at the Royal Oak and the end of your journey is now just a short stroll to your right.

Date walk completed:

Places of Interest Nearby
From Lincoln's by-pass the **Road Transport Museum** in North Hykeham is easily reached. The golden age of motoring is recalled by this collection of restored local cars, buses and commercial vehicles. Telephone 01522 500566 for details. Wildlife enthusiasts will enjoy **Whisby Nature Park**, a nearby area of lakes converted from former gravel pits into a conservation centre. Telephone 01522 500676.

The Royal Oak

Two of the most attractive stone-built villages between Lincoln and Sleaford are linked by this trek around the rich farming country of North Kesteven. The traditional country pub by the stream in Scopwick is your base, while the stunning estate village of Blankney occurs at the mid-point of the walk. Not one stone still stands on the haunting site of the once imposing Hall in Blankney, but there remains more than enough beauty and elegance in the splendid buildings around the village.

When it comes to enjoying a traditional pub meal and a relaxing drink no better place than the neatly mown banks of the stream outside Scopwick's **Royal Oak** could be imagined. This fine ivy-clad building of old stone and red pantiles offers delicious and unpretentious meals, including roast lunches on Sundays and home-made sponges and crumbles. A good range of lighter snacks and sandwiches is also on offer. Accompany your meal with a pint of Tetley's or one of the guest beers, such as Adnam's or Wells Bombardier.

Opening times are 11.30 am to 2 pm and 7 pm to 11 pm. Meals can be ordered every day from 12 noon to 2 pm and from 7 pm to 9 pm.

Telephone: 01526 320285.

Distance: *5 miles*

OS Explorer 272 (Lincoln) or Landranger 121 (Lincoln).
GR 067580

A mainly level walk on rural tracks and field paths.

Starting point: The Royal Oak in Scopwick. There is roadside parking on the opposite side of the stream and along Vicarage Lane, reached from the B1188.

How to get there: Scopwick is easily located midway between Lincoln and Sleaford on the B1188.

The Walk

1 Leaving the pub cross the river and set off towards the church. The centre of Scopwick is a delight. A series of small bridges cross the small stream, its surface rippled by ducks and shaded by draping willows. Rows of stone cottages and barns line the grassy banks. Alongside the churchyard turn into Church Row Passage and continue through the houses until you reach Vicarage Lane. Follow Vicarage Lane to the right, but not before you have visited the War Cemetery, where the graves of both Allied and German airmen lie side by side.

2 As the lane dwindles a clear grassy swathe, hedged by hawthorn on both sides, leads you off to the left and then to the right. This undulating 'green lane' is Trundle Lane and you remain on it to its end at Acre Lane. Look out for the sculpted wooden seat near to the water tank. This carving of a tree spirit is entitled 'Scopwick Woman' and was shaped from a single elm by Rosie Bradshaw in 1991. Turning left onto Acre Lane walk as far as the huge barns of Scopwick Low Field Farm.

3 Beyond the farmyard the route continues as a chalky track until it reaches a T-junction. Turn left and proceed along a similar track for half a mile. Just before the track bends right, towards another group of farm buildings, turn left onto yet another chalk track

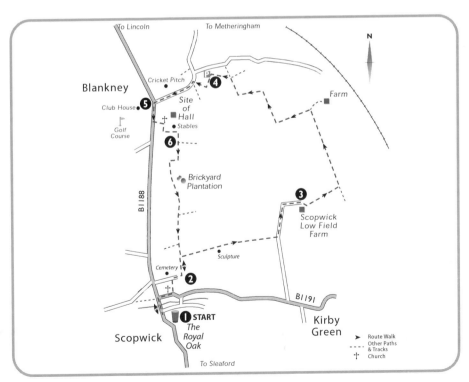

The village of Scopwick is a delight

which zigzags between the fields for a further mile. As you approach a road you will spy a stile in the hedgerow on your left. Over this is a meadow, on the far side of which another stile takes you into a small car park.

❹ Leave the car park not by the road but by a footpath on the far side, which joins the former trackbed of the private railway linking Blankney Hall with Metheringham – notice the handsome brick bridge hidden in the woods. Turn onto a path, opposite a stile on your left, leading through the wood to meet the road at a distinctive white gate. The village to your left is Blankney. There are footpaths leading into this estate village, but stay on the roadside to best enjoy the array of mellow stone buildings. Ornate gables, chimneys and turrets are everywhere, details are neatly picked out in the estate green and hedges are immaculately trimmed.

❺ Turn left at the main road, the B1188, and pass the grand entrance to the Hall before entering the churchyard of Saint Oswald's on your left. Beautiful in itself, the Victorian church conceals a sad history in the acres behind it. Though the stables still stand the towering stonework of Blankney Hall which once stood here has completely vanished – you may wander around to discover the bricks of original herringbone pathways still in place. Return to the church and cross the lawn to join the next driveway leading off the main road. Blankney's privileged surroundings continue as you follow this driveway behind the stables and past a charming brick house.

❻ Just past here do not follow the drive left where a sign reads 'Farm Access Road' but continue straight ahead onto a lesser track, sometimes heavy underfoot. This track bends this way and that before passing Brickyard Plantation on the left. Beyond here it is important to continue straight ahead, though better options may try to tempt you left and right. Finally, after a narrow stretch along the side of a field, you find yourself on Trundle Lane once more. Now retrace your footsteps for half a mile to arrive back at the Royal Oak.

Date walk completed:
....

Places of Interest Nearby
Scopwick is at the heart of 'Bomber County' and a number of World War II aviation heritage museums are close by. **Metheringham Airfield Visitor Centre** (telephone 01526 378270) and **Digby Ops Room** (01526 327503) are just two. **The Battle of Britain Memorial Flight** at Coningsby is also within easy reach.

The Blue Bell Inn

In the heart of the Lincolnshire Wolds a village which for 150 years has been the home of the South Wold Hunt is the setting for a very special inn and restaurant. From the inn in Belchford your walk follows valleys and streams to Scamblesby and Asterby, but the return is via an exhilarating high-level trail overlooking the best scenery that the area has to offer – even Lincoln Cathedral can be seen from here. Although the Wolds consist mainly of chalk much of this walk is on much older sandstone, which weathers to the greenstone used to build many of the region's churches.

Distance: *6 miles*

OS Explorer 273 (Lincolnshire Wolds South) or Landranger 122 (Skegness and Horncastle).
GR 293755

This is a challenging walk including steep gradients.

Starting point: The Blue Bell Inn in Belchford. You will be able to park by the church or in one of the nearby roads.

How to get there: Head north from Horncastle on the A153 in the direction of Louth. In 3 miles a road signed for Belchford leads off to the right and the village is just a mile along here.

The Blue Bell Inn has been immaculately restored and dazzling whitewashed walls, red pantiles and, of course, the most enormous bright blue bell arrest your gaze. This popular inn has placed the emphasis firmly on the quality of the food served. All menus are hand-written onto wall boards – including a separate vegetarian menu – and the choices range from exotic treats such as wild boar steak or rump of ostrich to favourites like Lincolnshire sausage and beef, Guinness and mushroom pie. On Sundays booking is essential for lunchtime meals, all of which are served with a Yorkshire pudding. Black Sheep, Wells Bombardier and Greene King IPA are amongst the choices of beer to accompany your meal.

Opening times are 11.30 am to 2.30 pm (12 noon to 4 pm on Sunday) and 6.30 pm to 11 pm. Meals are available from 12 noon to 2 pm (12 noon to 4 pm on Sundays) and from 6.30 pm to 9 pm. The inn does not open at all on Monday or on Sunday evenings.

Telephone: 01507 533602.

123

The Walk

1 Set off west from the Blue Bell Inn along the main road – do not stray into Ings Lane. In a couple of hundred yards a kissing gate on your right takes you onto the long distance footpath known as the Viking Way. Pursue this path running along the edges of two fields divided by a second kissing gate, then cross a footbridge in the hedgerow ahead to continue to another footbridge. Over this bridge the route shoots uphill across the meadow and targets the clear gap in the next hedge, beyond which a fenced track guides you along the lower slopes of Juicetrump Hill. This sandstone outcrop, believed by some to be a Neolithic longbarrow, appears here merely as a skyline copse.

2 Pass through three more kissing gates, keeping the ancient Belchford Wood on your left, before descending through the

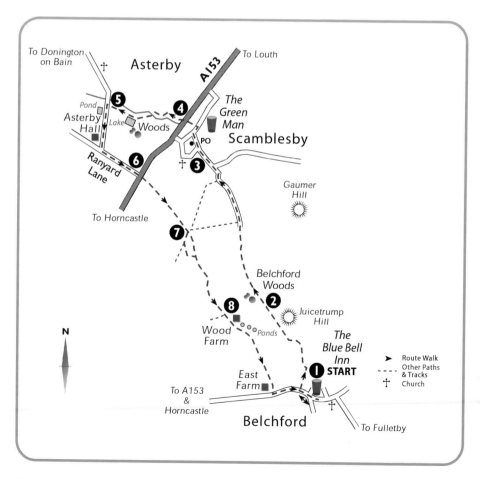

The Wolds viewed from the churchyard, Scamblesby

next meadow to join a firmer track at yet another kissing gate. Enjoying fine views up to Gaumer Hill and the Bluestone Heath Road on the right this road shortly joins Mill Lane, which now guides you into the centre of Scamblesby, uniting with South Street along the way.

3 Just before the charming little Post Office, still fitted with its original painted wooden shelves, conduct a circuit of the hidden core of the village by turning left into Church Lane. Along here you will come across the secluded turreted church, the old Vicarage and undoubtedly the area's finest conker trees! Now on Watery Lane turn right at the T-junction and continue in the indicated direction of Louth to pass a horse paddock on your left and cross the footbridge here. The

footpath you are on quickly reaches the main road, which you cross with care to continue on the far side, keeping the stream to your left.

4 This delightful grassy trail twists and turns alongside the bubbling stream, which it eventually crosses at a footbridge. Now with the stream on your right and its watermeadow to your left continue into the woods ahead, passing en route an enchanting tree-fringed lake, an ideal spot for weary limbs to rest.

5 Finally this waterside path comes to an end at the road near to Asterby, a delightful collection of farms and houses, and deserving of a brief exploration. The route proper, however, bids farewell to the Viking Way and continues in the opposite direction, climbing the hill to Asterby Hall and turning left here into Ranyard Lane.

6 When the main A153 is regained cross and proceed along the well signed bridleway that you will spot slightly to the left of the junction. Improving views now unfold and the way is clear along the borders of the first two fields and straight across the third.

7 Concentration is required at the meeting of ways in the hedgerow reached at this point. The right of way continues straight up the hill in your original direction, exactly as indicated by the signpost. Only if the path is not in place should you stray and follow the perimeter of this field to the right. Both alternatives aim for the clump of trees at the top of the hill, from where the footpath – still in the same direction – becomes clearer. The route now develops as a spectacular path along the edge of the plateau, offering exciting views down the escarpment and into the valley. A patchwork of colourful fields, wooded hillsides and the ancient cultivated terraces on the flanks of Gaumer Hill – this is the Lincolnshire Wolds at their finest. Still admiring the scarp views pass through a black gate, along a broad track and onto a surfaced lane beyond the next gates.

8 Now walk straight through the farm, passing on your left a block of brick holiday cottages and a chain of ponds tumbling down the hillside. Modifying to a grass track once more, your route also plunges downhill, exchanging positions with the hedge as it does so. Soon the surface improves to a gravel track and you continue straight ahead to the road, ignoring two attempts by the track to divert you into farmyards on the right. Turn left onto the road and stroll the final half-mile past the kissing gate and back to the Blue Bell in Belchford.

Date walk completed:
....

Place of Interest Nearby
Six miles south-east of Belchford **Stockwith Mill** near Hagworthingham is a picturesque watermill, whose wheel now turns once more after years of rest. As well as a fine tearoom and shop, the area's connections with Tennyson are well explained in an exhibition and trout ponds behind the mill are linked by a walk. Telephone 01507 588221.

The Black Horse

N o collection of Lincolnshire walks would be complete without an inclusion to dispel the popular belief that the county is entirely flat – and this is it. A steep climb up wooded hillsides to the top of the Wolds is rewarded by a breathtaking panorama of the surrounding hills and the valley of the River Bain below. The river itself forms part of the Viking Way, and as you follow its cascades and watermeadows you will come across an idyllic hamlet, two attractive lakes and a charming watermill.

Distance: 5 miles

OS Explorer 282 (Lincolnshire Wolds North) or Landranger 122 (Skegness and Horncastle)
GR 237828

This challenging route includes steep gradients. Very little road walking is involved.

Starting point: You will be able to park on the roadside in the village of Donington on Bain. The owners of the village shop may also allow you to park on their ground.

How to get there: Donington on Bain is situated midway between Louth and Wragby and is most easily accessed from the B1225 (the Caistor High Street). From here two clear signed roads lead into the village while signposts also indicate other minor roads linking the village with the A157 and the A153.

The **Black Horse** has long enjoyed an excellent reputation as a first class halt for food, drink and accommodation along the Viking Way. Relax in the tiny intimate bar at the hub of the inn before choosing from a warren of dining areas leading off. Your meal will consist of the finest local meat and produce, Lincolnshire Red Beef steaks are a speciality, and a choice of roasts supplement the menu on Sundays. Home-made treacle sponge and jam roly-poly are hard to resist, while vegetarians and children are also well catered for. A number of fine guest beers are rotated at the pumps and might include Theakstons Bitter and Greene King IPA.

Opening times are 12 noon to 3 pm and 7 pm to 11 pm. Meals are available from 12 noon to 2 pm and from 7 pm to 9 pm. The pub does not open on Monday lunchtime, however.

Telephone: 01507 343640.

The Walk

❶ Head south from the pub in the centre of Donington on Bain until you spot Simon's Close on your left. Just past here a signed footpath vaults a stile and makes for open countryside, with a hedge to the right and a series of meadows and horse paddocks on the left. Over another stile the way becomes steeper and more exposed, and superb views unfold over the wooded flanks of the Wolds hillsides and the Bain valley behind you. Soon the

track rises through one of these woods called Horsebottom Plantation before emerging as a chalk track and attaining the summit of the Wolds where four ways meet at a break in the hedge on the left. Look back over the plantation to view the cathedral in distant Lincoln, while ahead are the unearthly dismantled 'dishes' of the radar station.

❷ Turn left here onto a grassy track – muddy in parts – and enjoy this exhilarating high-level route until it

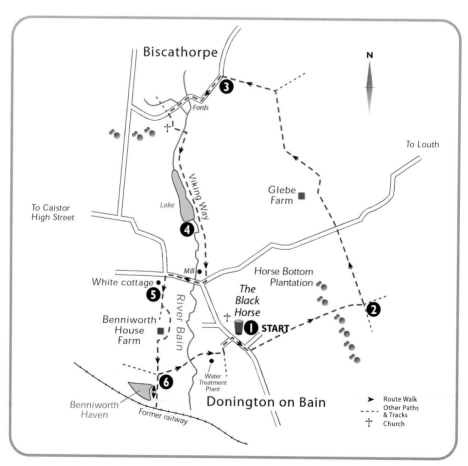

crosses a road and begins to lose height. Where this track reaches an attractive combe on the left be sure to locate the gap in the hedge and continue along the broad grassy track. Bearing right at a bend (ensure that the hedge remains to your left) then left onto a firmer lane you finally arrive at a narrow surfaced road onto which you turn left.

3 Now descend towards the shrunken medieval village of Biscathorpe. Spotting the hollow octagonal lantern of the tiny church – one of several such Victorian confections in the vicinity – look for a kissing gate at the far end of the churchyard wall. A narrow fenced footpath now leads you to a wooden bridge, beyond which you turn to the right and follow the reedy banks of the infant Bain.

4 Past a large tree-fringed lake your path crosses another footbridge in a copse before pursuing a field-edge path as far as a stile. A clear path across the next two pastures now leads you back onto a road by a pretty whitewashed watermill. The bridge overlooking the mill and the waterfalls is a good point to rest and admire this scene before continuing over the bridge and right, up the hill to a white cottage at the first junction.

5 Cross the cattle-grid on the left and follow this lane to a group of tall beeches and horse chestnuts. Before the next cattle-grid the right of way veers into the grass on the left, where you will see a signed gate beneath the horse chestnuts. The path is clearer beyond the gate and traces the lower perimeter of the farm buildings. Follow the hedge away from the farm, crossing to its opposite side via a hidden stile, and continue past a new plantation of oak to a gate in the corner of the field near to a derelict house.

6 Your route is over the stile by the gate, but first it is well worth exploring the narrow footpath ahead of you as far as the bed of the railway that once linked Wragby and Louth. Along here you may survey the serene lake of Benniworth Haven, surrounded by many species of shrubs and trees. Now head back to the gate and over the stile. Head down the pasture to the River Bain once more. Now cross the footbridge and the nearby stile, pass the water treatment plant and cross the track after clearing another stile. A narrower path now leads you past the woodyard and a small field before a fenced passageway takes you as far as a lane back amongst the houses in Donington. Turn left onto this and right at the next junction – soon enough the Black Horse comes into view at the end of the lane ahead of you.

Date walk completed:

....

Places of Interest Nearby
The nearby market town of **Louth** is a fascinating place to spend a few hours exploring the many speciality shops, narrow passageways and regular markets. The town's museum has been expanded to include William Brown's acclaimed **Louth Panorama** and the spectacular spire at 295 feet makes this the country's loftiest parish church. Telephone Louth Tourist Information Centre on 01507 609289 for more information.

typical Marsh villages. Curiously, two of these each possess two parish churches within yards of each other. The walk may at times be a good test of your route-finding ability but the views towards the nearby hills of the Wolds are rewarding, especially from the walls of the elevated reservoir.

The broad level plain of the Lincolnshire coastal marsh has a lighter and altogether distinct flavour from the fens in the south. This circuit around the region takes in a lengthy section of the disused Louth Navigational Canal and visits three

Distance: 7 miles

OS Explorer 283 (Louth and Mablethorpe) or Landranger 113 (Grimsby)
GR 338945

A level walk on mainly good surfaces.

Starting point: The New Plough in Covenham Saint Bartholomew. Ask in the pub for permission to leave your vehicle or park on the side of the road to the north.

How to get there: Head north from Louth on the A16 towards Grimsby. Just past the Fotherby by-pass the turn-off to Covenham is on the right. Continue through the village until the New Plough is reached on the left. Minor roads also lead into the village from several other directions.

The New Plough is one of two excellent pubs serving food in the village. It enjoys a charming rural setting opposite the leafy churchyard of Saint Bartholomew's. Recently redesigned in a more contemporary style, the lounge and dining area are comfortable and cheerful. The meals lean heavily on local produce and are all freshly cooked to order. Favourites include Lincolnshire sausage with spring onion mash and haddock in beer batter. The filled baguettes are a speciality and roast Sunday lunches are so popular that you are advised to book in advance. In addition to Bateman's XB and Carson's Cream a guest beer such as Greene King IPA is always available.

Opening times are 12 noon to 2 pm Wednesday to Saturday; 5.30 pm to 11 pm Monday to Saturday; 12 noon to 10.30 pm Sunday. The inn is closed Monday and Tuesday lunchtime. Food is available between 12 noon and 2 pm Wednesday to Saturday and 6 pm to 9 pm Tuesday to Saturday; 12 noon to 8 pm on Sunday No meals on Monday evening.

Telephone: 01507 363284.

The Walk

1 Head north from the New Plough and, as you leave the village, turn right at Barn Owl Cottages into Grange Lane, signposted as a bridleway to Grainthorpe. Past a succession of farms the grass ramparts of Covenham Reservoir come alongside. Further along here a long flight of steps may be ascended to view the reservoir and the vast panorama encircling you. The spire in Louth and the Lincolnshire Wolds are clearly seen. You should not, of course, approach the water's edge.

2 When Grange Lane arrives at the Grange itself follow the signed track around the right-hand edge of the farmstead and stay on this grassy lane as it passes a fascinating selection of old farming implements. When the lane peters out cross the field on your right diagonally (or walk round the edge if the path is absent) targeting the substantial railed footbridge over the Louth Navigational Canal. Cross this bridge and immediately turn right to proceed along the east bank of the canal (signed for Austen Fen).

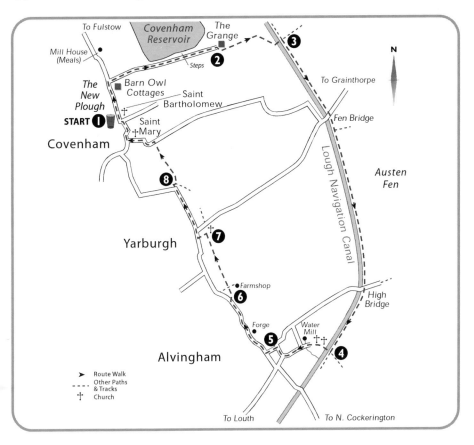

The watermill at Alvingham

❸ This delightful waterside path, lined with hawthorn full of bright red berries, is now your companion for a full three miles, enjoying more expansive views over the coastal marsh and the Wolds. Swans and moorhens glide by, and the remains of derelict locks can be distinguished along the canal. Two roads are crossed en route, one at Fen Bridge, next to a handsome brick warehouse, and a second at High Bridge, a pleasant farming hamlet.

❹ Approaching Alvingham you may rub your eyes in disbelief as you study the church in the trees ahead. But there really are two churches in the same churchyard, reputedly the closest in the country at a mere twenty paces. One, in fact, is the parish church of nearby North Cockerington, but oddly it is the one nearest Alvingham. Alvingham's church is unique as England's only dedication to Saint Adelwold. Cross the canal by the footbridge to enter the churchyard and then pass through a farmyard, on the other side of which the charm is maintained by a picturesque watermill, beautifully preserved in full working condition. Now make you way along Church Street to the village stocks and branch right into High Bridge Lane.

❺ Turn left into High Street then right into Yarburgh Road at the t-junction. As you leave the village you will come across a restored blacksmith's forge, a barn topped by a curious glass turret and galleon weathervane, as well as the day's only uphill stint!

6 Reaching a brick house with a veranda on your right turn into the track and immediately clear a stile on the left to embark upon a section requiring close attention in following the route. Those suffering from navigational nervousness may choose to remain on the road, both options aim for the embattled church tower in Yarburgh. Back on the field footpath two more stiles take you over the drive leading to the farmshop. More stiles in the next meadow appear to serve no purpose whatsoever, but stiles marking the entry and exit points of the following four fields need to be located exactly. Eventually along a short track and across a narrow lane, only a horse paddock protected by an electric fence (easily sidestepped!) stands between you and the churchyard in Yarburgh.

7 Having inspected the imposing weathered church at close quarters, leave the yard by returning to the main road and continuing to the right in your original direction towards Covenham. The footpath shown on OS maps as continuing across the fields is not so much challenging as unfathomable, and can be recommended only to the most obstinate of ramblers.

8 Where the road bends sharply left, just past a yard guarded by four strange Jeeves-style figures, it is safe to cross the footbridge on the right and rejoin the footpath. Keep the ditch on your left over the first two fields then cross another bridge, beyond which your path leads clearly over the final two fields and down to the road. Turn left to re-enter Covenham and fork right at the only junction, noting that, for the second time on the walk, two churches occur in very close proximity. Your starting point at the New Plough is now just around the corner from Saint Bartholomew's, the second of these churches.

Date walk completed:

....

Places of Interest Nearby
Don't forget to visit **Alvingham Farmshop** passed on the walk between Alvingham and Yarburgh. Telephone 01507 327205 for times. At **Rushmoor Country Park** in North Cockerington near Alvingham, a collection of rare and ornamental species of poultry can be found, plus a tearoom and a shop. Telephone 01507 327184. More wildlife can be seen nearby in November and December when hundreds of grey seals come ashore to breed at **Donna Nook**.

Two of North Lincolnshire's least known but most fascinating villages are linked by this tranquil

Distance: *7 miles*

OS Explorer 281 (Ancholme Valley) or Landranger 112 (Scunthorpe and Gainsborough)
GR 972999

This walk is a blend of all types of terrain from narrow field paths to open road walking - and not a hill in sight.

Starting point: The village green in Redbourne. Park around the green or ask in the pub for permission to leave your car in the car park.

How to get there: Redbourne is situated on the B1206 five miles south of Brigg, and can also be easily reached from the A15 (Ermine Street) a mile to the west.

excursion close to the River Ancholme. Wide views extend to the hilly Wolds in the distance, and the lofty towers of the churches of both villages are prominent throughout. Both Waddingham and Redbourne are full of handsome stone buildings, but Redbourne enjoys a particularly illustrious history dating back to medieval times and the Grand Falconers of England. This is all in addition to a restored coaching inn serving delicious food and its own exclusively brewed beer.

The setting of the **Red Lion** opposite the towering beech trees on the large village green is impressive indeed, and it looks every inch the traditional coaching inn with its striking black timbers and archway leading to the former stables. A comprehensive range of meals and snacks is on offer – the chef's 'Really Good Fish Pie' is popular. On Sundays, however, a carvery replaces all menus. Choose between the Duckpond Bar and the more elevated ambience of the restaurant. All areas are newly refurbished in a tasteful contemporary style, and are the ideal place to enjoy a pint of the exclusive Duckpond Bitter, made locally by Tom Wood's brewery.

Opening times are 12 noon to 11 pm every day except Sunday (10.30 pm). Meals are served everyday between 12 noon and 2 pm (2.30 pm on Sundays) and from 6 pm to 9 pm in the evening.

Telephone: 01652 648302

The Walk

1 Redbourne is full of features of charm and interest, and looking around these may well delay the start of your walk. From the Red Lion stroll to your left, passing the tiny fire station in which the village's original horse drawn fire engine of 1831 is proudly displayed, to the gurgling beck where ducks splash on willow shaded pools. Arriving at the far end of the large green cross the main road and enter School Lane. Here a curious restored smithy, still housing the old forges, is surmounted by a prancing white horse. Having passed a stone arch (part of the Victorian school, and not connected with the earthworks of the former castle which lie in these grounds) School Lane enters an area of new housing. Here locate a fenced footpath beside a distinctive mock lych gate which leads you towards another lane of stone houses.

2 Instead of following this lane where it crooks to the left turn onto a footpath entering an arable field on the right, and continue in more or less your original direction, signposted for the River

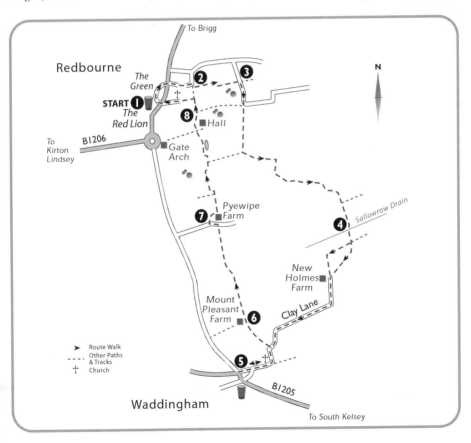

The arched gatehouse leading to Redbourne Hall

Ancholme and keeping the beck on your left. The path briefly enters a wood via a footbridge before tracing the edge of a private lawn as far as a surfaced road – turn right onto this.

❸ At a sharp left turn branch right onto a lane indicated as a dead end, where a footpath sign to Sallowrow Drain will confirm your route. The track you now find yourself on is quite delightful, and you continue along it for 1½ miles, until the track rises suddenly to cross a ditch before heading off to the left. At this point leave the track and continue straight ahead across the slightly rising field in front of you, at the highest point of which two marker posts at the substantial bridge crossing Sallowrow Drain come into view.

❹ At the bridge you will spot another marker post on the far side of the next field – if the footpath is not in place skirt the right hand edge of this field – either way you arrive at another farm track, which you follow to the right. After a bend to the left you soon reach New Holmes Farm, where the track improves to a metalled lane. This is Clay Lane, which now snakes between the fields for over a mile enjoying superb views towards the approaching village of Waddingham, until it reaches the old stone rectory and the village church. It is well worth continuing through the rows of fine stone houses until you arrive at the large green in the centre of Waddingham. A wayside stream, a village pub and a prominent school bell-turret of 1830 add charm to this scene. There is also a village shop if your supplies require replenishing.

5 Now it's time for the return journey – begin by retracing your footsteps past the church and along Clay Lane as far as the first bend to the right. Here a narrow field-edge footpath leads off to the left. Along here look carefully for more signposts guiding you through the nettles of the next short difficult stretch. Another perimeter path and a clear way through the crop of the following field then lead you up to the rambling buildings of Mount Pleasant Farm.

6 Join the clear track leading north from the farm and at a lone oak tree continue straight ahead into a meadow, in the far right hand corner of which, a footbridge in the trees takes you back onto arable land. A few yards to your left a grassy swathe, clearly identified by a row of telegraph poles, now guides you all the way to a substantial hamlet called Pyewipe Farm. At the farm join the road and follow it to the left until you reach the last houses on the left.

7 Here, on the other side of the road a footbridge leads you onto a broad mown path taking you behind the farm buildings before shooting left into open countryside once more, keeping a lofty hedge to its right. When it turns sharply to the left do not follow this track but continue ahead once more on a mown path, which performs a zigzag before heading north

towards the nearby belt of tall trees. Entering the woodland follow the track you now find yourself on to the right and out of the trees, then remain on it as it twists past a new plantation. Look for the plaque commemorating a local farmer, and the English Holly planted here by his family. When you espy the Great Fish Pond on your right leave the track and continue straight ahead once again on a lesser path. The ornate Gothick gate arch to your left is well seen from here, though a post-walk viewing at close quarters is strongly recommended. The driveway leading to the splendid Redbourne Hall is soon crossed, and here a sign indicates the continuation of your grassy path.

8 Rounding the corner of a garden containing a puzzling ecclesiastical ruin and mock cloisters, look for a signpost to Little Redbourne and follow in that direction. A short distance along this path another sign (for Vicarage Lane) diverts you to the left across one last field towards the extraordinarily tall tower of the church. Enter the churchyard by a kissing gate and leave via the main path, where Vicarage Lane guides you back to your starting point in the centre of Redbourne. The village sign bears a wealth of information about the history of the village, especially concerning the Dukes of Saint Albans, who carried the hereditary title of Grand Falconer of England.

Date walk completed:

Place of Interest Nearby
Two miles west of Redbourne **Mount Pleasant Windmill** is a traditional tower windmill in full working order. Having observed the organic flour being ground on a tour of the mill you can sample the cakes and bread in the tea rooms, or buy them from the wholefood shop. Telephone 01652 641077.

History and mystery shroud the Isle of Axholme, an undulating oasis in an otherwise flat and once swampy expanse by the mighty River Trent. Your hike through entirely agricultural countryside leads you from a shrunken port – significant enough in medieval times to boast its own castle – to Epworth, the home of John and Charles Wesley and the birthplace of world Methodism.

The White Hart is a welcoming hostelry just yards from the River Trent, on whose banks you can sit and enjoy your refreshment in fine weather. The lounge overlooking the river is full of fascinating photographs of old Owston Ferry and the Aegir, the Trent's own tidal bore. The fare concentrates on traditional favourites such as steak pie and Grimsby haddock, while the home-made sponges and Sunday roasts are particularly delicious. Lighter snacks for the less hearty eater are also available and, as you would expect in this agricultural heartland, most produce used is locally sourced. Fine ales like Theakston's Coolcask and Black Sheep supplement the usual beers on offer.

Distance: *7½ miles*

OS Explorer 280 (Isle of Axholme) or Landranger 112 (Scunthorpe and Gainsborough)
GR 814000

A walk on mainly level terrain, but footwear should allow for some sections of field walking and muddy tracks.

Starting point: The White Hart on North Street in Owston Ferry. Park in the Market Place or on the High Street.

How to get there: Owston Ferry lies on the west bank of the River Trent midway between Crowle and Gainsborough, and can be reached by leaving the A18 at Althorpe near Scunthorpe and following the river. Two signed roads also link the village with the A161 at Haxey and Epworth.

Opening times are 12 noon to 11 pm Saturday and Sunday; 5.30 pm to 11 pm Monday to Friday, plus Thursday 12 noon to 2 pm. Closed other weekday lunchtimes. Meals are served from 12 noon to 2 pm Thursday, Saturday and Sunday; and 5.30 pm to 9 pm every day.

Telephone: 01427 728206.

The Walk

1 Walk from the White Hart into Owston Ferry's former Market Place and on into the High Street. Of many interesting buildings the most intriguing is the old smithy, now a museum of the village's heritage run by friendly volunteers and open to the public on Sundays and bank holidays. Eventually you arrive at a turreted stone archway bearing coats of arms and weathered sculptures. Through this is a lych-gate leading into a churchyard, with Saint Martin's in front of you and the earthworks of a motte and bailey to the left – all that remains of a castle once held by the powerful Mowbray family but destroyed in the late 12th century. Having inspected both church and castle leave the yard by a kissing-gate on the far side of the church.

2 Back on the road turn back towards the village but almost immediately turn left into Church Walk. Turn left again at the t-junction onto a lane that leaves the houses and climbs gently away from the Trent, revealing extensive views over Haxey and the surrounding lowlands.

3 At High Burnham turn right in front of the farm as directed by a wooden footpath sign onto a clear track over the fields. Keeping to the hedgerow as it kinks first left then right the route later makes its way through a field of crop. The way is clearly identified by a series of yellow markers. At one point the path joins a track which leads you to the left before infuriatingly doubling back in a copse to resume its original progress north. If in doubt, ensure that a disused windmill tower on the horizon is your goal. A sequence of field paths, tracks and hedgerows now follow

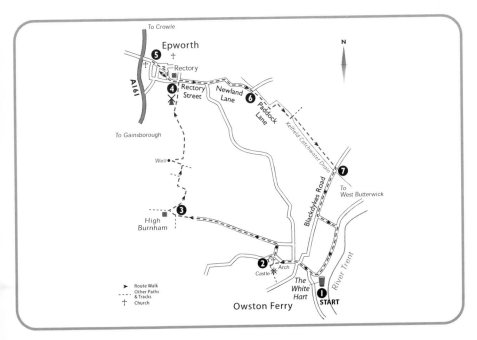

The old rectory at Epworth was once Wesley's home

5 Now reverse your footsteps back to the rusty gate, this time continuing along Rectory Street until it pivots to the right, where you branch left into Newland Lane to re-enter arable country. Reaching a new brick house (not shown on OS maps) continue straight ahead onto the grassy track known as Paddock Lane.

6 Once more guided by the yellow waymarkers remain true to the wide drainage channel now on your left. Even when Paddock Lane crosses and departs from the drain your path continues along its opposite bank.

7 After a mile your waterside trail ends abruptly on Blackdykes Road. Turn right onto this then left in a further half-mile into another lane leading directly to the raised levee of the River Trent. Turn right to follow the riverside road – the bank may be ascended briefly to gain views over the Trent to Laughton Forest and Hardwick Hill. If you are fortunate you may even witness the tidal bore known as the Aegir surging along the Trent. Now simply continue along this road for half a mile to find yourself back at the White Hart in Owston Ferry.

before the brick shell of the windmill tower is passed and, at a rusty gate, you find yourself on a road with the historic little town of Epworth to your left.

4 Even if time is limited a thorough exploration of Epworth should not be omitted. Just past the Old Rectory, John Wesley's family home, turn right into Albion Hill to pass a statue bearing his famous words 'I look upon all the world as my parish'. In the Market Place pass the steps of the cross from which Wesley delivered many rousing sermons and continue along the High Street to the Memorial Methodist church built to the memory of the Wesley brothers. Saint Andrew's church also contains features linked to the family, while next door is the site of Epworth Manor House, the seat of the Mowbrays first encountered at the castle in Owston.

Date walk completed:

Places of Interest Nearby
Sandtoft Transport Museum, 4 miles north-west of Epworth, is a nostalgic collection of preserved trolleybuses – phone 01724 711391 for details of 'Trolley days'. At nearby **Haxey** on 6th January each year huge crowds gather for the traditional tussle for the Haxey Hood, a form of rugby dating back 700 years.

After the cathedral in Lincoln itself Thornton Abbey is arguably Lincolnshire's most spectacular architectural treasure. Founded by the Augustinians in 1139, the Abbey's imposing gatehouse still displays finely carved figures set into the high façade niches. It is difficult to believe that so close to the blighted industrial landscape around Immingham such a tranquil and rural ramble as this can be enjoyed. Impressive brick-built farms and houses may be admired throughout this journey around the fields, woods and lakes surrounding the Abbey, to which a short drive is required from the inn.

Though the hounds and horses of the **Thornton Hunt** last met many years ago the name lives on at this typical village inn. Delightfully situated opposite the yard of the ancient church, and in the shadow of its swaying beeches, the inn's unspoilt interior is adorned with hunting scenes. Here home-made favourites include cottage pie with a cheese and leek topping and traditional puddings such as jam roly-poly. Roast lunches are added on Sundays and a full range of lighter snacks and children's meals are available. In addition to Mansfield Dark and Tetley's you will always find a guest beer from Tom Wood's brewery, Bomber County for example.

Opening times are 12 noon to 3 pm and 6.30 pm to 11 pm (Sunday 7 pm to 10.30 pm). Meals are available from 12 noon to 2 pm (2.30 pm on Sundays) and from 7 pm to 9.30 pm (9.15 pm on Sundays).

Telephone: 01469 531252.

Distance: 5 miles

OS Explorer 284 (Grimsby, Cleethorpes and Immingham) or Landranger 113 (Grimsby).
GR 114190

A walk on rural tracks and footpaths, but including two short sections of roadside verge walking.

Starting point: The walk begins at Thornton Abbey's small car park, and the inn is the Thornton Hunt in nearby Thornton Curtis.

How to get there: Thornton Curtis is situated 5 miles south-east of Barton upon Humber on the A1077, which also links with the A18 and the A180 in the opposite direction. The route from the inn to the walk's starting point can be found in the notes for the walk.

The Walk

1 To reach the start of the walk drive south from the pub on the A1077. Turn left into Station Road as you leave Thornton Curtis, continue past Thornton Abbey Station and turn right at the t-junction by the level crossing – from here the car park at the Abbey ahead cannot be missed. From the shadow of the mighty gatehouse, stride north along the road in the direction of East Halton. The verges are fairly narrow and care is required.

2 Around the first corner (noting the ancient fish ponds on your right) turn left, when you reach Thompson Ground. Here three successive gates guide you along the drive, across a small field and

onto a good track which passes a dense briar patch. The path becomes more narrow and exposed as it twists and turns along the field boundaries, but a series of yellow waymarkers, which you will spot around the entire journey, confirms your route. A clear path across a field of vegetables now takes you to a cluster of buildings, whose surfaced driveway leads you in turn to the road in Goxhill South End.

3 At this point the architecturally inquisitive should stray left to inspect the nearby 14th century hall known wrongly as Goxhill Priory. Otherwise head to the right, along the road, before branching right again into the first lane, signposted both as a public footpath and a dead-end. A number of interesting buildings are

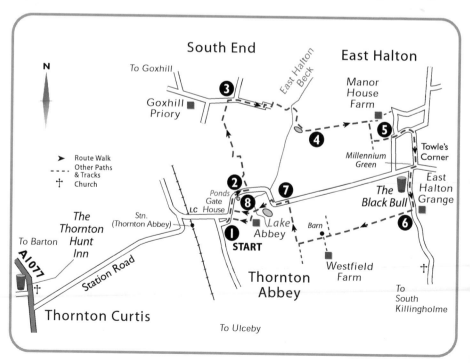

The spectacular Thornton Abbey

passed along this winding lane before it terminates at a farm. Here the clear footpath traces the left-hand edge of the farm, wends past a coppice of slender stemmed saplings (grown apparently for weaving) and crosses a wooden footbridge over the East Halton Beck. Now follow the far bank to the right before your trail veers left through this rather untamed landscape to pass a pond on the right, fringed by tall trees.

4 Suddenly the terrain changes and you find yourself on a broad open farmtrack between fields of crop. Pursue this invigorating track for a good half-mile to reach the gate opening into the trees surrounding Manor House Farm. Abandon the track at this point and turn right onto the footpath along the

hedgerow. Midway across the second field a footbridge on your left leads you alongside another hedge and onto the roadside in East Halton.

5 To best enjoy a circuit of the buildings of old East Halton continue straight ahead along King Street then turn right when you reach Townside. Arriving at the Millennium Green on Towle's Corner turn left to pass the village shop and the Black Bull public house.

6 When you reach East Halton Grange, on the left a bar gate on the other side of the road opens onto another footpath. This long straight track now cuts across the countryside for an enjoyable mile. Where the sheltering hedge on the right breaks, fine views of Thornton Abbey and the distant Humber Bridge unfold. Briefly uniting with a road serving the nearby farm, the route – still unerringly straight – joins a field edge path at a black barrel-shaped barn. Finally a wooden gate signals the end of this stretch and a wide rutted track takes you to the right and back to the road. The view of the Abbey from this track is sensational. Even the Chapter House, normally considered a lesser fragment, looms large from here.

7 Exercising suitable care once more turn left onto the road and, part way around the bend, dive left at a hidden sign to enter the final – and most rewarding – section of the walk. Skirting a large pond on your left, dense reed beds and bulrushes around its edges, spot an elaborate if rickety footbridge crossing the East Halton Beck. Past here another bridge, identical to the first, leads you to a clear path running along the edge of a field, at the end of which is a third bridge and the road ahead. At this point the car park is a short distance to your left – and

the chance to fully explore the precincts of the gatehouse and Abbey.

8 However, between the first two of the three bridges, you may have noticed a path through the meadow which crosses the stonework of a small ancient bridge and leads directly to the gate of the fenced remains of Thornton Abbey. These remains are open to the public, free of charge and a thrilling finale to the day's outing. Excellent information boards help to plug the gaps in your knowledge and, having thoroughly absorbed the history and the atmosphere of the ruins, a finer walk than that across the pasture to the magnificent gatehouse could not be imagined. Finally through the half-rotted oak timbers of the mighty doors and along the barbican the car park is reached – it is worth remembering that these gates are closed daily at 6 pm.

Date walk completed:

....

Places of Interest Nearby

Nearby Barton upon Humber's rope, brick and tile making heritage is charted in the **Ropewalk**, which also houses a quality craft shop and art gallery. This historic old town also boasts a remarkable Anglo-Saxon church, a viewing area for the Humber Bridge and the start of the Viking Way. Contact Brigg Tourist Information Centre on 01652 657053. In the Abbot's Garden at **Thornton Abbey** you will find a 'Maize Maze' in summer

return
slender
second helpings

Text copyright © 2012 Carol Bowen Ball
Design and layout © 2012 Bariatric Cookery (UK) Ltd
The rights of the author and publisher have been asserted.

First published in 2012 by Bariatric Cookery (UK) Ltd,
Stamford Place, Crawley Drive, Camberley, Surrey, GU15 2AB
www.bariatriccookery.com

Cataloguing in Publication Data: a catalogue record for this
book is available from the British Library.

ISBN: 978-0-9566626-1-3

Designed by Andrea Rumsey, RumseyShort
Kings Court, 91-93 High Street, Camberley, Surrey, GU15 3RN
www.rumseyshort.co.uk

Printed by Aaron Printing Ltd

Contents

Foreword

Welcome to 'Return 2 Slender....second helpings'. Here is the companion book to the original 'Return to Slender' bariatric cookbook. It offers yet more recipes for the weight-loss surgery patient, but also additional advice on things like eating out, 'mindful' eating, wise shopping choices, stepping up the exercise and that red flag warning...regain (and what to do about it!) which weren't covered in great detail before. My hope is that it will be just as warmly received as the original.

I have been delighted and often humbled by the terrific response I got to my first bariatric cookbook. I knew there was a need for a UK book but my travels to support groups nationwide, messages on social media like Facebook and Twitter, response to my monthly newsletter, and missives on my website and in my inbox have all verified that as a group we are poorly supported...so we help ourselves. Thankfully, many professionals in the bariatric field felt the same, so I am most grateful to those surgeons, bariatric nurses, dieticians, psychotherapists and, most of all, patients (and their families), for their feedback and support.

"'Return to Slender' is a must-have book for any bariatric patient wanting to learn how to make delicious recipes for themselves and their families."

Mr Chris Pring, Consultant Bariatric Surgeon

Sadly, obesity is still very much on the increase and there are few solutions that offer major long-term success. Bariatric surgery does have a substantially better outcome than most diets for those who are morbidly obese and now offers major savings for the NHS and other agencies.

Unfortunately, when the world economy is in a strangle-hold, funding will be scarce, regardless of the figures.

My work hasn't changed substantially over the last couple of years, other than the fact that it is more in the headlines... I still want to help bariatric patients restore a good and normal relationship with food so that they enjoy and appreciate all meal occasions. I endeavour to do this by relaying some tried and tested advice (based on my own and others experiences in the UK but also with my work based in the USA, where they have a longer track-record with bariatric surgery and its complexities); some flavoursome and WLS-friendly recipes; and perhaps by encouragement, promotion, networking and publicity.

I hope I can rekindle enthusiasm in those who thought they would never eat normally again, and encourage those who thought they couldn't control their eating to some degree, that they can...with variety, good food choices, superb nutrition and support.

Carol Bowen Ball

Before you begin...

This book takes over where 'Return to Slender' left off and is intended as an additional resource for those who have had bariatric (weight-loss) surgery. You are strongly urged to read the first book relating to the food stages involved; advice on fluids; information on vital vitamins and nutritional supplements; stocking up on the best ingredients; tips and advice from a dietician; useful equipment to make the going easier; suggestions for exercise; and advice on cooking after surgery, as vital background information.

Eating right with every bite – let's recap

 1st 'Fluids' stage

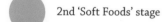 2nd 'Soft Foods' stage

 3rd 'Eating for Life' stage

The recipes in this book have been colour-coded to make identification and selection easy according to your stage of eating. If the recipe has been colour-coded as suitable for your current stage then it can be considered for your eating plan, although in some cases it may need to be puréed before serving.

We recognise that people's food tolerances vary enormously so only you will know what you can eat and when you can attempt a food or recipe. Your bariatric team will also give advice and their recommendations should be followed above all others.

The nutritional analysis breakdown of the recipes is just the same...giving information on calories, protein, carbohydrate and fat. They are all based on the normal or average (rather than weight-loss surgery) portion size. This is because portion sizes do vary greatly over time from early surgery days to many years down the line. It's easy to check your quantities e.g. if you eat half the normal / average portion then halve the calories, protein, carbohydrates and fats, likewise if you only eat a quarter of the normal / average portion then divide the quantities by four.

Recipes are also coded for suitability for freezing ❅ and for vegetarians by this symbol Ⓥ

Slim pickings

I used to think that grocery shopping would be a doddle after WLS. If I'm not eating so much and cooking less then my trolley dash would be so much faster, wouldn't it? Well no. What I didn't factor in was my new need to choose much more carefully than before, check labels, scrutinise back-of-packs and seek out better alternatives for my new bariatric regime. In an effort to make your shop a speedier and more nutritious one, here are some of the things I have learnt and sensible swaps I have made.

Supermarket sweep!

First and foremost go to the supermarket with a firm idea or list of things that you want and stick to it. Temptation comes in all guises and if once off-the-list-items are in your basket and at home then they are generally consumed rather than wasted. The same goes for shopping on a full stomach…you are less likely to make unwise choices if you don't feel hungry.

"Carol's book is my bariatric bible…the book travels with me everywhere from support group to supermarket."

Barbara, Gastric Bypass Patient

Know your store layout too (although I know they keep changing) to keep things on an even keel. Remember that skirting the store is the best place to find fresh produce so keep to the periphery. Processed and junk type foods are generally located in the centre aisles. I avoid them and never miss the tempting offers! Likewise keep your eyes down and make a determined effort to get through the checkout before the snacks, sweets and treats call out to you.

If you're looking for a bargain then look below your eye-line to the lower shelves… this is where the basic, economy and essential produce is stored. And never, never, ever believe the hype on lite / good-for-you / healthier-than-ever jargon or claims until you check the back of pack to verify whether the protein is high, the fat low and the sugars (rather than carbs) are acceptable for the portion size. Remembering, of course, that a WLS portion is generally much smaller than that recommended on a pack and that our requirements for high nutrition in a few spoonfuls must be met.

Bariatric swap shop

Over the last two years I have sampled, tasted and evaluated a good many products (with many, many claims) and here are some swaps I think are worthy of consideration.

Sugar for sweetener: I don't add sugar, occasionally use honey but have become quite adept at substituting sweeteners when required in recipes. I have used a good number from Splenda granulated, agave nectar to xylitol and use them where they perform best.

Low-fat cooking sprays and a little good-quality oil for cooking: Sometimes the former saves me countless calories and keeps the fat levels low in a dish or recipe and at other times the judicious use of a little high-quality oil makes all the difference. When flavour counts, opt for the latter, when calorie saving is important then spritz away. If you want to make your own version, simply place a little oil in a spray bottle with water (and perhaps add herbs and spices) shake well before spraying onto food or a pan to use. Store in the refrigerator.

Skimmed and semi-skimmed milk for full-fat: Protein and calcium levels stay the same in the lower fat alternatives so it's a no-brainer choice for me. Skimmed alternatives behave just as well in recipes and general cooking but can save countless calories and bring the fat level down to an acceptable level.

Yogurts in all their glory: I've tasted so many low-fat (but high-sugar) variations that I mistrust this category more than most. My solution to all is to use a fat-free Greek yogurt and to flavour or sweeten it myself...works on every level.

Low-fat spreads and light butters for the real thing: Again for most recipes I will opt for the former to reduce the calories and fat...but when flavour is paramount and portion size is very small... indulge in a little.

Lighter than light mayonnaise for the real thing: I used to think this was a hard thing to give up, but not so. I now readily use the former and even sometimes make it lighter still by mixing half and half with fat-free Greek yogurt in sauces and salad dressings.

Low, half-fat and reduced-fat cheeses: This category presents itself in all its glory and misery! Some half-fat and low-fat cheeses are good and many low-fat soft / cream cheeses are brilliant, yet some are soapy, artificial and quite horrible. Rather like protein drinks, breakfast bars and other diet solutions you may find one or two that you are happy with. A great deal of the time I prefer to opt for a strong-tasting medium-fat alternative and use less of it because the flavour is intensified, rather than the lower-fat alternative. It will be a question of taste. Quark, found in the chilled cheese cabinet, will also offer a very low-fat alternative to cream cheese.

Frozen or canned for fresh alternatives: I have never quite understood the prejudice and preference for fresh over frozen produce, especially when quality and nutrients might be compromised. Many frozen alternatives have a better nutrition profile than their fresh but 'stored' counterparts. So you will find a whole host of frozen vegetables and fish in the **www.bariatriccookery.com** freezers for recipe development and family eating. Likewise, some canned items can outstrip their fresh equivalents, when it comes to convenience, ease of use and versatility.

'Convenient' alternatives for ready-meals: I am no martyr when it comes to putting a meal on the table mid-week. My time is also valuable and sometimes I don't want to spend hours at the chopping board, hob or oven! I advocate looking for convenient alternatives rather than buying a ready-meal. Check out your salad bar and rôtisserie in the supermarket. For example, here you can buy the makings of a great stir-fry that will knock the socks off any ready-made stir-fry meal. Likewise, let someone do the hard and time-consuming preparations for you…buy chopped vegetables, fruits, cooked rice / lentil sachets without the guilt. You're onto a winner with time and flavour! I also recommend using ready-made pastes, prepared and mixed seasonings and lazy ingredients like chopped ginger, garlic and chilli for speed and other sensational flavours from a jar!

Passata or creamed tomatoes in stews and casseroles: Stock up on these cartons or flavoured jars of tomatoes… they are indispensable in chillies, bolognese-style sauces and casseroles. No need for thickening!

Puréed beans to thicken dishes: Purée a can of beans like kidney, cannellini, butter or flageolet and use to thicken a dish rather than add flour or cornflour / *cornstarch*. You're adding extra protein and nutrition!

Whey protein powders and skimmed milk powder to boost the protein profile: There are a few, but only a few, flavoured whey protein powders that I take occasionally as a drink, most are far too sweet and artificial for my palate. I do however use an unflavoured one and sometimes skimmed milk powder (when the flavour suits) to stir into soups, sauces, casseroles and other cooked dishes to raise the protein profile more frequently. Most days I reach my 70g protein target without the need for a protein powder or skimmed milk supplement but if you consistently fall short this might be something to consider.

"Great talk by Carol Bowen Ball tonight at Chelsfield – 'Return to Slender' lady. If you ever get the chance to go to a group where she is the speaker, don't miss it!"

Beverley, Gastric Bypass Patient

Eating out

One of my greatest worries pre-op centred around eating out post-op. I needn't have been too concerned for I happily dine out at least twice a week these days and in countless venues with varied cuisines. I have however a few tips which I hope you will find useful when navigating your way through menus and food situations.

All you can eat...

No I am not just talking about buffet spreads and eat-as-much-as-you-can diners but specifically about eating right with every bite because it won't necessarily be very much. I find it helpful to:

- Check the menu before arriving so that my food selection will be wise. Most places post them on an internet site or position outside the eatery for viewing.
- Ask for a smaller plate or use my side plate to maintain portion control. A large plate can overwhelm and invite attention when much is left uneaten.
- Pace myself with my fellow diners by putting my knife and fork down between mouthfuls, chewing well and finishing at about the same time.
- Go off menu! I frequently have two starters rather than a starter and a main meal; ask for a children's portion; or request a take-home bag. Sometimes I simply just say it's unlikely I will eat all my portion so could you 'bag' half of it before bringing to the table.
- Ask for sauces and dressings on the side. Ask for the chef to cook with the minimum amount of fats and sugars and decline the usual bread basket.
- Try to observe the no drinking 30 minutes before and after my meal.

- Consider a card (like the ones produced by BOSPA) that you can hand to the waiter which requests that because you have had surgery to reduce your stomach size, could you be allowed to order a small-sized meal from the main menu or children's menu. It's a good discreet way of managing food ordering when out with those you don't know too well or are unaware of your surgery.

I have found most eating places are happy to do all of the above and if they don't...I don't go there again!

So what can I eat when dining out?

These days, even fast food outlets have some healthier choices than years ago, so there is generally something for everyone.

Burger bars and drive thrus: grilled / *broiled* chicken or vegetable salads, burgers without the bun (discard), oats / porridge and fruit salads are fine every now and again as a 'treat'.

Sandwich bars: look for meat and salad selections on wholemeal breads or in wholegrain low-carb wraps. Avoid those with lashings of cheese and mayonnaise. If you choose a salad make sure the dressing is on the side and you can choose to have a little or ditch it.

All you can eat buffets: This can be your best or worst option, depending upon self-control and wise or foolhardy food choice. Always do a quick survey of what's on offer before starting to fill your plate. Focus on the protein whether it be a roasted meat, cold deli platter, bean-based curry or seafood selection then add a few vegetables, salad or fruit and finally a carb-based accompaniment. Eat in the same order for a great dining-out option.

And for international cuisine?

Mama Mia Italian: Best bets on the list of antipasti / starters are soups like minestrone and salads (although ask for the dressing on the side). For the main course choose grilled / *broiled*, roasted or braised fish, chicken or meat. Pasta is good providing it is with a tomato-based rather than creamy sauce but go steady with the grated cheese. Forget Italian pizzerias, although if nothing else is available choose a thin crust. Instead cook one at home.

The Real Greek: Greek meze like grilled / *broiled* calamari and hummous can be a good choice especially if you have vegetables for dipping. Grilled / *broiled* or baked seafood and souvlaki make an excellent dinner selection. A Greek salad can also be ideal but again hold on the dressing. Forget Greek desserts, most are calorie laden…ask for fruit instead.

Choosing Chinese: This can be a real challenge since many foods are deep-fried or drowning in sweet sauces. Look for dishes that contain steamed or stir-fried vegetables, steamed or roasted seafood or tofu with vegetables. A great choice to start is hot and sour soup. Go easy on the noodles with any dish and eat with chop sticks to slow things down.

Indulging in Indian or South Asian: These can be good eating venues since much of the cuisine is based on vegetables, pulses, chicken and fish. Tandoori chicken, prawns Madras and fish kebabs make an excellent option as well as lentil dhal and vegetable curries (made without creamy sauces). A spoonful or two of basmati rice should suffice.

Try Tex-Mex: Many of these dishes are heavy on cheese, refried beans, sour cream and tortillas so it is probably best to cook these from scratch at home so that you have control over the ingredients. Instead look for grilled / *broiled* seafood, chicken or meat with salsa or dishes made with beans (but not refried). Gazpacho soups are fabulous, so too ceviche.

Tempting Thai: A tricky place this…since many of the sauces used are sweet and made with full-fat coconut milk or creamed coconut. Try dining on a lemongrass broth type soup, Thai beef salad, a vegetable stir-fry or satay chicken dish.

I think I'm turning Japanese! There are lots of wonderful options once you get beyond the sushi and tempura. Order sashimi, a clear vegetable or miso soup, sukiyaki or grilled / *broiled* fish.

Mindful eating

Have you discovered the difference between real hunger and 'head hunger'? Knowing the difference between emotional eating and feeding for nourishment begins with learning to care for yourself (and accepting that negative feelings can and do pass). Crucially however, it requires learning to manage your emotions in ways that don't involve food. So, not easy!

We often mistake emotional hunger, whether it is tiredness, stress, boredom, anger or anxiety related, for being hungry. So how can we stop ourselves from making a bad day seem better by relying on and fixing things with food?

First check if you're really hungry

Ask yourself these questions to find out if you're really 'hungry' in the real physical sense or just 'hungry for something'.

- Is my stomach rumbling? Can I feel real physical symptoms of hunger?
- Could I simply be thirsty? Hunger and thirst produce similar symptoms in the body.
- Is this a sudden attack of hunger or has it been gradually growing over a few hours?
- Have I eaten in the last 3-4 hours?
- Is this a sudden or urgent need to eat?
- Has my mood suddenly changed?

Experts think that if you answer 'yes' to the final three questions, then the chances are that you are eating or wish to eat to fill an emotional rather than physical need. In other words, not real hunger!

So what can I do?

Six ways to stop eating for the wrong reasons

1. Distract yourself: This is a great way to buy time. It could be something practical like gardening, reading, knitting or ringing a friend. Or it could be a pleasurable mental activity like planning a special holiday or weekend away. Or it could be an emotional activity like flicking through an old photo album or watching a favourite comedy show on TV.

2. Learn self-soothing: Each time you go to eat something ask yourself 'What's this all about?' This will encourage you to be mindful around food...whether you're eating for the right or wrong reasons. Then ask yourself 'What else would make me feel better?' Would it be better to have a relaxing bath, go for a walk or text a friend? Learn to soothe yourself with food-free treats and activities.

3. Spot your emotional eating triggers:
Keeping a food diary that includes the situation, place and company in which you ate, and how you felt before, during and after eating can be most illuminating. Getting to know your 'enemies' will help you to discover that certain situations, people, events and feelings are triggers. Once you know what these are you can put in place coping mechanisms to deal with them.

4. Establish a regular eating regime:
This isn't about going on a diet but more about having three regular meals and perhaps a couple of small snacks. Nor is it about skipping meals…this is a way of ensuring that the body is well nourished and that real hunger can be identified and learned.

"Carol understands, like only a WLS patient can, the challenges that bariatrics face when trying to cook healthy and nutritious meals for themselves and their families. We know you will benefit from her recipes and advice whether you are pre or post-op surgery."

Mr Shaw Somers and Mr Guy Slater, Bariatric Surgeons and TV's 'Fat Doctor'

"Carol I refer to your book and website almost daily for inspiration, especially when I get a little bored with what I am eating."

Gemma, Duodenal Switch Patient

5. Choose food you enjoy: If you are only going to be able to eat a little, and with WLS that is the aim, then ensure it is food you like and eat it slowly, savouring every bite. Don't eat too quickly, rarely tasting the food or just to numb emotions. Eat at a table, with cutlery, with no distractions – not in front of the TV. Sit down to eat, rather than re-fuel on the hoof.

6. Be kind to yourself: Being self-compassionate and accepting that you have emotions can be difficult and scary, but is the first step towards being more relaxed around meals. This is the first rung on the ladder towards having a better relationship with food.

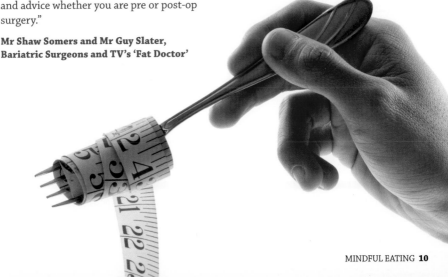

Upping the exercise

Undoubtedly you will be advised to increase your activity levels before surgery. This is for two main reasons; firstly it will make the transition to exercising after your operation more manageable; and secondly it can make the surgery easier by decreasing your levels of body fat and weight.

Then, after surgery and your initial post-op rest days, you'll be encouraged to pick up on activity, little by little, until by about six weeks you should be able to comfortably manage a gentle (not strenuous) work out. This is important because exercising after WLS dramatically improves the results you experience from your procedure.

Honey I shrunk myself!

So basically it's now over to you. You've been given an amazing tool to work with food-wise, but you can ensure this works superbly well by building more activity into your life, for great weight-loss and maintenance.

If you've never exercised before or at least not on a regular basis then there are a few precautions for safety you'll want to note.

Seven tips for exercising safely

1. **Start off before surgery.** For the reasons already mentioned above.

2. **Begin with walking.** Walking in short increments is a great way to start toning up the muscles and preparing your body for future exercises.

3. **Discuss exercise with your bariatric team.** They will know specifically when you are ready to move on and increase your exercise and will also inform you about any specific risks to consider.

4. **Do 5-15 minutes of cardio exercise before strength training.** Strength training is ultimately what will help you increase and gain muscle mass but it's always a good idea to warm up your body with a short cardio workout.

5. **Start off with 1-2 sets of 6-15 repetitions.** Start small and build up gradually never putting your body under undue stress in the early days. As you get stronger you will be able to endure more.

6. **Don't overdo it with the weights.** Don't strain yourself, use just enough weight to feel a little resistance.

7. **Keep a diary of your workouts.** A workout diary can be just as useful as a food diary in helping to keep you on track, monitor your progress and highlight your successes which can be very motivating.

So what is the best kind of exercise?

A question I glibly asked a personal trainer...the reply? 'The one you will do!'

Ah yes, no point taking out an expensive gym membership if you won't go; likewise forget swimming if you don't like getting your hair wet! Fortunately there are many different ways to add activity to your day. One is bound to suit your personality, wallet and ability.

Most bariatric teams will recommend starting with walking, swimming and aqua classes (providing all wounds have healed), cycling and low impact exercise equipment. Later down the line you may be able to consider abdominal training, yoga, resistance training and more cardiovascular focused workouts.

However:

Small daily ideas = big difference

- Try walking or cycling rather than using the car.
- Get off the bus one stop before your destination and walk the rest.
- If you like walking consider a pedometer. Record your steps and try to increase 10% each week aiming eventually for 10,000 steps per day.
- Hide your remote and get up out of the chair to change channels.
- Walk your dog or a neighbours daily.
- Use the stairs rather than the lift.
- Walk up the steps on an escalator.
- Go up and down the stairs as often as possible during the day, rather than stock-piling items at the bottom.
- Get a Swiss ball and sit on it when using the telephone or watching TV to master balance and improve core strength.
- View housework and gardening as a workout rather than a necessary chore.

Recommended types of exercise

For **aerobic** consider walking, dancing, swimming and cycling. For **non-weight bearing** consider water-based aerobic exercise or recumbent bicycling until you become fitter. **Resistance exercise** is very beneficial. Choose exercises that are comfortable and that you can perform in a pain-free range of motion. Free weights, machines and exercise bands can all be used to increase your strength. If you are inexperienced then ask a professional to show you how to perform the exercises correctly. Rotate your workouts to avoid overuse / pressure on joints.

For how long?

Work towards 5 x 30 minutes of activity a week. To start with this may mean 3 x 10 minute blocks of activity like walking. Build up slowly. Have patience and realistic expectations.

For the best results experts suggest that you have a focus; set yourself some goals; make exercise a top-of-the-list priority; have a support system or buddy for when the going gets tough; plan well so that you know what you are going to do and when and have a 'can-do' attitude; have balance and keep things manageable by remembering the slow-and-steady wins the race rather than the race-to-the-tape; be accountable by keeping a progress or score sheet; and finally be consistent…think of exercise as a long-term lifestyle change and choose activities you will enjoy.

"An invaluable book for the WLS patient and good resource for many bariatric professionals. Carol has also given great help to our bariatric team at their support group…we always welcome her return."

Mr Roger Ackroyd, Bariatric Surgeon

Slim chance

Many, many people are wildly successful with WLS but this usually doesn't happen by accident. They haven't been blessed with the 'magic wand' of success but usually have found a regime that helps them to reshape their body, mind and spirit so that they lose their excess weight and maintain the loss.

Most WLS patients will experience a 'honeymoon' period after surgery, when hunger is virtually non-existent and the pounds or kilos fall away rapidly. Then reality sets in…hunger often returns and with it a return to all the old destructive behaviour patterns that threaten long-term success.

Not everyone returns to these old behaviours though and some briefly experience them and take evasive action through personal responsibility to put them right. Recognising the red flags that can cause regain is helpful so here's a list of the most common ones, along with some tips to help you regain-proof your WLS.

"Carol's sharing of her weight-loss journey in our patient support group, provided real insight on how to be successful following bariatric surgery."

**Jacqueline Kurt, Dietician,
Derby Hospitals NHS Foundation Trust**

Red flags

There are three main ones. Recognise these and take immediate action:

- Snacking on soft carbs.
- Grazing rather than having a three meal and two snack a day regime.
- Eating too many soft / slider foods.

AND PERHAPS FOR SOME (IF YOU HAVE BEEN TOLD NOT TO):

- Drinking with meals.

There are countless reasons for going back to these old habits but most relate to thinking they are harmless; they're comfortable and comforting; and they are readily available. In isolation or together they can signal REGAIN.

Think of red flags as tools…warning tools, just like the surgery itself. Recognise them and make changes as quickly as possible so that you don't hit a plateau or start to regain. You are more likely to correct any destructive behaviours if you are aware of them.

"This is an excellent book…not just for the recipes but also as a helpful guide to the changes that need to be made after WLS."

Zoe, Gastric Band Patient

Tips to regain-proof your WLS

- **Don't avoid the scales:** Know what you weigh so that you are accountable before things get out of hand. A weekly weigh-in is a good way of avoiding denial and staying conscious.

- **Move:** If the quantities of food that you now eat have increased or you're choosing higher density / calorie options then the best strategy to maintain your loss is to move more. More exercise will compensate for the calories you have added back into your diet. Of course the best solution might be to cut back on those foods but if you find you can't then this is the next best thing.

- **Record what you're eating and drinking:** Most studies show that those who write down or record their food and drink intake, have the best chance of making wise food choices and experience positive weight management. It's not by accident...they are keeping on track because they are conscious of their good and bad food choices.

- **Treat your depression or addictions:** Many people who have had WLS suffer from depression or addiction and this doesn't miraculously disappear along with the excess weight. Treating these is a positive step forward, ignoring it can undermine your WLS success.

"Carol, the evening was a resounding success and the feedback has been fantastic. Thank you for visiting us, everyone enjoyed the talk and the lovely food, 'very inspiring' was what one girl described you as."

BOSPA Support Group Leader, Goring Hall Hospital

- **Follow expert advice:** From time to time it's very useful to revisit the guidelines your surgeon, bariatric nurse, dietician, psychologist and medical practitioner gave you. It's easy to forget the basic advice that holds true. Likewise open your mind to new advice and update your guidelines. New motivational information can be most uplifting when you're way down the weight-loss surgery journey.

- **Seek help:** Sounds simple but not everyone does. Help can come from the most surprising places so don't close your mind to support groups, responsible and monitored on-line forums, buddy schemes and therapy groups. It can be a good idea to familiarise yourself with these before you may need them.

Up bright and early
Some ideas for breakfast...

Everyone seems to agree that breakfast after weight-loss / bariatric surgery is a must. It jump-starts your metabolism for the day and breaks the food and drink 'fast' of overnight thereby nourishing and hydrating your body. The choices below (colour-coded to suit the stages after surgery) are good because they introduce a lot of protein, are quick and easy to prepare and some are portable for taking away from home when pressed for time.

- Thin porridge made with skimmed or semi-skimmed milk.
- Instant cereal made with skimmed or semi-skimmed milk.
- Weetabix saturated with skimmed or semi-skimmed milk.
- Fruit smoothie diluted to a thinnish consistency.
- Slimfast type shake.
- 'No-added sugar' fruit juice diluted with water.
- Low-fat and low-sugar whey protein isolate shake or protein drink.
- Milky chai type tea or low-fat and low-sugar chocolate type drink.
- Vanilla egg custards.

All the options opposite and:

- Lightly-scrambled egg on wholemeal toast.
- Crackers with low-fat cheese spread.
- Corn or bran flakes saturated with skimmed or semi-skimmed milk.
- Low-fat and low-sugar yogurt or fromage frais with mashed banana.
- Lightly-cooked soft omelette.
- Melba toast and Marmite or low-fat cheese spread.
- Soft-boiled egg with wholemeal toast.
- Very soft fruit compôte without added sugar.

All the options opposite, above and:

- Wholemeal toast with low-fat spread and sugar-free jam, pure fruit purée, Marmite or smooth peanut butter.
- Any 'no-added-sugar' breakfast cereal with skimmed or semi-skimmed milk.
- Porridge with fruit e.g. strawberries or blueberries.
- Shredded Wheat with dried fruit and skimmed or semi-skimmed milk.
- Fresh fruit salad with low-fat fromage frais.
- Poached egg and wholemeal toast.
- 2 egg omelette with mushrooms or other vegetables and / or low-fat cheese.
- Small portion low-sugar baked beans with wholemeal toast.
- Grapefruit segments, a baked egg and wholemeal toast.
- Low-fat and low-sugar cereal bar.

- Home-made low-fat and low-sugar breakfast muffin.
- Low-fat and low-sugar muesli or granola with skimmed or semi-skimmed milk.
- Vegetable and cheese frittata.
- Cottage cheese or low-fat ricotta cheese pancakes.
- Baked French toast made with wholemeal bread.
- Baked or grilled / *broiled* full-English breakfast with egg cooked in low-fat cooking spray.

Sweet potato soup

This wholesome, chunky soup can be assembled in minutes, especially if you use frozen diced sweet potato. It makes a very satisfying lunch or supper dish with its cheese and seed topping, although it is just as delicious without. The soup can also be puréed to a smooth consistency for those in the early eating stages after surgery.

Calories: 310
Protein: 18.9g
Carbohydrate: 41.8g
Fat: 8.2g

SERVES 4
WLS portion: ½

Metric / *US*
low-fat olive oil cooking spray
½ tsp chopped red chilli
2 leeks, chopped
600g / 1¼lb sweet potatoes, peeled and diced or 500g / 1lb frozen diced sweet potatoes
900ml / 3¾ cups vegetable stock / *bouillon*
410g / 14oz can chickpeas, rinsed and drained
salt and freshly ground black pepper
125g / 4oz reduced-fat Halloumi cheese
2 tsp mixed seeds
2 tbsp chopped fresh parsley

1. Generously spritz a large pan with the low-fat cooking spray, heat gently then add the chilli and leeks and cook for 5 minutes until softened. Add the sweet potatoes and cook for a further 3 minutes.
2. Add the stock / *bouillon* and bring to the boil. Reduce the heat, cover and simmer for 5 minutes. Add the chickpeas and salt and pepper to taste and cook for a further 5 minutes.
3. Meanwhile, drain the cheese then dice and pat dry on kitchen paper. Spritz a small non-stick pan with low-fat cooking spray, add the cheese and cook gently for 1 minute. Add the seeds and cook for a further 1-2 minutes or until the cheese is just beginning to colour.
4. Blend the soup to crush the vegetables (but don't fully purée unless in the very early stages of eating after surgery). Ladle into bowls and scatter the top with the cheese and nut mixture. Sprinkle with the parsley to serve.

A light bite
Some ideas for lunch...

One of the most popular requests I receive is to suggest some meal ideas for lunchtime eating, be it at home, away at work, from a lunchbox or on the move. Here are some that you might like to consider. A wide-necked flask or microwave will cope with most hot options and an insulated lunchbox will take care of the chilled ones.

- Small cup of clear or puréed soup.
- A low-fat and low-sugar smoothie.
- Puréed or well-mashed smooth avocado with seasoning.
- Mashed or puréed smooth tofu with vegetarian gravy.
- Tender cooked lentils or dhal thinned to a runny consistency.
- Smooth type cup-a-soup.
- Very gently set egg custard.
- Bariatric-friendly whey protein isolate drink or shake.
- Low-fat and low-sugar sorbet or ice cream.
- Low-fat and low-sugar mousse or yogurt.
- Low-fat and low-sugar custard with a little smooth puréed fruit.

All the options opposite and:

- 2-3 tbsp fish + mashed potato + vegetables blended with a low-fat cheese sauce.
- 2-3 tbsp minced meat / *ground meat* / casseroled meat / curried meat + mashed potato or pasta + vegetables blended with gravy or sauce.

- 2-3 tbsp cauliflower cheese blended with mashed potato.
- 2-3 tbsp dhal blended with low-fat yogurt
- Small bowl of smooth or soft chunky soup blended with extra vegetables, cheese or yogurt.
- Wafer-thin meat and soft salad vegetables with low-fat dressing and breadsticks.
- Baked beans on crispy toast.
- Low-fat soft cheese or pâté with crispbreads, tomato and cucumber.
- Poached or scrambled egg on toast.
- Omelette with cheese or cooked vegetable filling.
- Cottage cheese and crackers or crispbreads.
- Couscous salad with meat, fish or vegetables.
- Low-fat hummous or other bean dip with Melba toast or breadsticks.

All the options opposite, above and:

- Jacket potato with topping such as baked beans, flaked tuna, grated low-fat or cottage cheese.
- Wedge of frittata or Spanish omelette with a little salad.
- Portion of crustless quiche with a little salad.
- Small portion of stir-fried vegetables with meat, fish or Quorn if liked.
- Wholewheat pasta with a tomato-based sauce.
- Grilled fish fingers with a little mashed potato and peas.
- Brown rice or wholewheat pasta salad with chopped meat or flaked fish, tomatoes and a low-fat mayonnaise.

- Mackerel or sardines on toast.
- Wholemeal bread sandwich, pitta or wrap with meat, fish, cheese, egg or vegetable mixture and salad.
- Low-fat sausage + grilled tomatoes and mushrooms.
- Meat, fish or vegetable kebabs with a little brown rice.
- Small salad with meat, fish, eggs, beans or cheese.

Three cheese bake

This recipe has three cheeses in it but it also scores on three levels...it tastes fantastic; is great at breakfast, brunch or lunch; and has a whopping 15.7g protein per WLS portion! It's also good hot, warm or cold (so perfect for lunchboxes and picnics).

Calories: 290
Protein: 31.4g
Carbohydrate: 14.2g
Fat: 12.4g

SERVES 4
WLS portion: ½

Metric / *US*
low-fat cooking spray
6 eggs
25g plain flour / *¼ cup all-purpose flour*
1 tsp baking powder
salt and freshly ground black pepper
1 tbsp snipped chives
175ml / *1 cup* skimmed milk
225g / *1 cup* low-fat plain cottage cheese
125g / *4oz* low-fat soft cheese, cubed
100g / *1 cup* cubed low-fat mature / *sharp* Cheddar
  or hard cheese
2 tomatoes, sliced

1. Preheat the oven to 180°C / 350°F / gas mark 4. Generously spritz an 18 x 23 cm / *7 x 9 inch* deep baking tin or similar dish with low-fat cooking spray.
2. Beat the eggs with the flour, baking powder, salt and pepper to taste and chives.
3. Add the milk, cottage cheese, soft cheese and hard cheese, mixing well. The mixture at this stage will look 'lumpy' but does cook to a smooth and creamy consistency.
4. Pour the mixture into the dish and top with the sliced tomatoes. Bake in the oven for 35-45 minutes until well-risen, golden but still wobbly in the centre. Remove from the oven and allow to stand for about 15 minutes before serving.

Smooth operators

In the early days after weight-loss / bariatric surgery you may need plenty of fluid 'meal-in-a-glass' type options. Later on you may want a quick fluid / smoothie choice to replace a meal during the day or just something to ensure you're hydrated. Here they are...my smooth operators!

Tropical fruit smoothie with vanilla ice

Metric / US

Place the diced flesh of about ⅓ pineapple in a blender with the diced flesh of ½ mango and 150ml / ⅔ cup tropical fruit juice (without added sugar) and process until smooth. Serve topped with a scoop of low-fat and low-sugar ice cream or frozen yogurt.

SERVES 2
WLS portion: ½ - ¾

Calories: 160
Protein: 2g
Carbohydrate: 32.5g
Fat: 2.3g

Beetroot, pomegranate and orange smoothie

Metric / US

Place 100ml / *generous ½ cup* pomegranate juice in a blender with 100ml / *generous ½ cup* orange juice (without added sugar) and 1 cooked beetroot / *beet* and process until smooth. Serve at once plain or over ice.

SERVES 1
WLS portion: ½ - 1

Calories: 110
Protein: 2g
Carbohydrate: 26.7g
Fat: 0.1g

Root juice

Metric / US

Place 1 chopped raw beetroot / *beet*, 2 chopped carrots, 10 French breakfast radishes, 2 cored and chopped apples and the flesh of ½ lemon in a juicer and process. Chill the juice before serving.

SERVES 2
WLS portion: ½ - 1

Calories: 88
Protein: 2.9g
Carbohydrate: 28.8g
Fat: 0.6g

Fruity radish juice

Metric / US

Place 2 cored and chopped apples, 2 cored and chopped pears, 3 chopped sticks / *stalks* celery and 10 radishes in a juicer and process. Chill the juice before serving.

SERVES 2
WLS portion: ½ - 1

Calories: 107
Protein: 1.6g
Carbohydrate: 32.5g
Fat: 0.4g

Protein smoothies

There is no doubt that it is better to get your protein from food rather than supplements. However, some of us just can't get the 70-100g recommended level on a daily basis and constantly fall short. This is where a protein drink can bridge the gap. One drink can supply about 24g protein! There are copious brands around and it is only by tasting that you will know if they hit the spot or not. I find many just too overly sweet. I really like the Syntrax Nectar range. Make up with milk for added protein and add a little frozen or fresh fruit to lift to a fresher level.

Parma ham, strawberry and mozzarella salad with a kiwi dressing

Here is a salad with two of my most favourite ingredients, strawberries and Parma ham. It's a wonderful combination enhanced with an unusual kiwi and lime dressing, all the better for devouring in the summer sun!

Calories: 168
Protein: 11.8g
Carbohydrate: 11.2g
Fat: 8.7g

SERVES 4
WLS portion: ½

Metric / US
350g / 12oz ripe strawberries, halved
125g / 4oz pack half-fat mozzarella cheese, sliced or torn apart
25g / 1oz walnut halves, hand crushed
a handful of fresh basil leaves, roughly torn
4 slices Parma ham, halved
Dressing:
2 kiwi fruit, peeled
zest and juice of ½ lime
2 tbsp fat-free French dressing

1. Arrange the strawberries, mozzarella, walnuts, basil and Parma ham on 4 serving plates.
2. Purée the kiwi fruit in a blender and sieve to remove the seeds. Add the lime zest, lime juice and French dressing, mixing well. Drizzle over the salad to serve.

Portable portions

I receive so many requests for ideas for lunchboxes or meals away from home that I think they would make a book on their own. These are a few I recommend...

Bariatric bean salad

Metric / US

Bring a pan of water to the boil, add 100g / 4oz fine green beans and cook for 2-3 minutes. Drain and refresh under cold water then cut into bite-sized pieces. Mix the green beans with a 400g / 14oz can drained borlotti beans, a 400g / 14oz can drained cannellini beans, 1 finely sliced red onion and 100g / 4oz crumbled reduced-fat feta cheese. Spritz liberally with a low-fat balsamic dressing spray to serve.

SERVES 4
WLS portion: ½

Calories: 170
Protein: 14.2g
Carbohydrate: 20g
Fat: 3.8g

Coronation chicken

Metric / US

Mix 75ml / ⅓ cup extra-light mayonnaise with 75ml / ⅓ cup fat-free natural or mandarin yogurt, 2 tsp curry paste, grated rind and juice of 1 orange, 1 tsp grated fresh ginger and 1 tsp finely chopped red chilli (optional) to make a smooth sauce. Add 4 diced, cooked, skinless and boneless chicken breasts, 1 finely chopped red onion, 4 chopped soft dried apricots, 1 peeled and chopped mango and salt and pepper to taste, mixing well. Serve garnished with chopped fresh coriander / cilantro.

SERVES 4
WLS portion: ½

Calories: 245
Protein: 30.9g
Carbohydrate: 19.5g
Fat: 4.8g

A cheesy salad choice

Metric / US

Cook 225g / 8oz plain or wholemeal pasta shapes in boiling, salted water for 10 minutes or as directed on the packet. Drain and refresh under cold running water. Mix the pasta with 50g / 2oz raw or cooked diced baby corn, 50g / 2oz diced cucumber, 50g / 2oz halved cherry tomatoes, 50g / 2oz thawed frozen peas and 100g / 4oz chopped half-fat hard cheese. Meanwhile, mix a 150g / 5oz pot fat-free Greek yogurt with 1 tbsp reduced sugar tomato ketchup / *catsup* and salt and pepper to taste. Fold into the pasta mixture to coat evenly.

SERVES 4
WLS portion: ½

Calories: 285
Protein: 20.2g
Carbohydrate: 39.2g
Fat: 5.2g

Portable feasts

Whether you are eating at work or on the go, it's important to keep meals not only high in nutrition but also interesting, with a variety of flavours and textures, so that boredom doesn't set in. Weight-loss surgery patients can't rely upon the staple sandwich of old but can mix and match a whole host of dishes like soups, salads, wraps and fruit skewers to ring the changes on a daily basis.

Salads needn't be the usual greenery but can be based on pasta, rice, quinoa, couscous, barley or potato. Soups can be summery light to wintery hearty; cold or piping hot; chunky or velvety smooth. Wraps can hold spicy bean mixtures, protein-packed meats, cheese or fish and the soft flour tortilla can be replaced with a lettuce wrapping if preferred. Fruit skewers offer seasonal variety that knows no bounds.

Supplement these with some ready-made bean-pots; pots of low-fat fish or meat-based pâtés with breadsticks; little packs of nuts; a low-sugar cereal bar; a small bag of mixed seeds; flavoured cottage cheeses and mini Babybels; and a few olives or dill pickles, and you have the makings of a pretty fine feast.

Turkey Korma kebabs

This curry inspired kebab recipe is easy to prepare and once made (ideally up to a day ahead for ease and good flavour) can be speedily cooked for a warming, guilt-free main meal. Serve with a fresh tomato and onion salsa and cucumber raita if liked.

Calories: 243
Protein: 40g
Carbohydrate: 6g
Fat: 6.5g

Cucumber and mint raita: Mix 6 tbsp finely chopped cucumber with 2 tbsp chopped fresh mint, 8 tbsp natural low-fat yogurt and salt and pepper to taste. Serve garnished with a sprig of mint if liked.

SERVES 4
WLS portion: ½

Metric / US

1 clove garlic, crushed
2 tsp turmeric
2 tsp garam masala
100ml / *generous ½ cup* hot water or chicken stock / *bouillon*
25g / *1oz* creamed coconut
150ml / *⅔ cup* natural low-fat yogurt
salt and freshly ground black pepper
600g / *1¼lb* thickly-cut turkey breast steaks
6 small onions, peeled and quartered
low-fat sunflower oil cooking spray

1. Put the garlic, turmeric and garam masala in a bowl and mix well. Mix the water or chicken stock / *bouillon* with the coconut then stir into the spice mixture. Allow to cool then stir in the yogurt with salt and pepper to taste.
2. Cut the turkey into bite-sized chunks, add to the yogurt marinade and mix well. Cover and refrigerate for at least 4 hours but ideally overnight.
3. Thread the onion quarters and turkey pieces onto 8 skewers and spritz each about 3 times with low-fat sunflower oil cooking spray.
4. Heat either a grill / *broiler* or griddle pan. Place the skewers either on a foil-lined grill / *broiler pan* or place on a griddle pan and cook for about 6 minutes.
5. From the grill / *broiler*, turn the kebabs and re-spritz again with low-fat sunflower oil or spritz the kebabs in the griddle pan once they have been turned over. Cook for a further 5 minutes or until the turkey is cooked through. Serve hot.

Quickies!

One eye on the clock and a meal to have on the table quickly? Then these are the recipes for you. Relying upon quick-cooking methods like stir-frying and griddling, they also tap into special spice mixtures and store cupboard and chill cabinet favourites for depth of flavour. They also depend upon prime quick-cook ingredients for success that you might pay a bit more for, but since you are eating less of them they become somewhat more affordable. Still cheaper than the local takeaway!

Super stir-fried chicken

Metric / *US*

Cut 2 large, skinless and boneless chicken breasts into thin strips and spritz generously with low-fat Oriental stir-fry spray oil. Heat a wok or frying pan, add the chicken and stir-fry for 3-4 minutes. Add 6 trimmed and sliced spring onions / *scallions*, 100g / *4oz* mange tout / *snow peas*, 1 trimmed and thinly-sliced leek and 1 carrot cut into julienne sticks. Spritz again and stir-fry until tender but still crisp. Serve on cooked noodles or rice.

SERVES 4
WLS portion: ½

Calories: 170
Protein: 27g
Carbohydrate: 8.5g
Fat: 2g

Speedy creamy salmon pasta

Metric / US

Drain 2 x 213g / 7½oz cans red or pink salmon, reserving 3 tbsp / ¼ cup of the liquid. Break into chunks. Cook 250g / 8oz pasta shells in boiling, salted water for 10 minutes. Meanwhile, cook 1 large finely-sliced leek, 100g / 4oz broccoli florets and 175g / 6oz fine green beans in boiling, salted water for 4 minutes, then drain thoroughly. Drain the cooked pasta, return to the pan with the reserved salmon liquid, vegetables, 2 tbsp chopped parsley and 250g / 8oz fat-free Greek yogurt. Stir over a low heat for 1-2 minutes, adding the salmon chunks at the last minute. Season to taste before serving hot.

SERVES 4
WLS portion: ½

Calories: 421
Protein: 32.3g
Carbohydrate: 50.8g
Fat: 9.7g

Spicy steak fajitas with tomato salsa

Metric / US

Spritz 300g / 11oz prime rib-eye lean steak with low-fat cooking spray then rub with 15g / ½oz Mexican fajita spice mix. Cook on a griddle or frying pan for 2-3 minutes each side until medium rare. Set aside to rest for 5 minutes. Griddle 4 low-carb and low-fat tortillas, one at a time, for 15 seconds until lightly coloured. Keep warm. Slice the steaks diagonally into thin slices and divide between the tortillas. Top each with some finely-sliced Little Gem lettuce, 1 tbsp reduced-fat tomato salsa, 1 tbsp grated half-fat Cheddar cheese, generous 1 tbsp fat-free Greek yogurt and 1-2 tsp chopped fresh coriander / cilantro. Roll up and serve at once.

SERVES 4
WLS portion: ½

Calories: 206
Protein: 23.7g
Carbohydrate: 14.8g
Fat: 8.8g

Bariatric fried 'rice'

I love a good fried rice. But these days rice can be a bit problematic. So here's my answer...a fried 'rice' made from cauliflower...yes seriously! One that is flavoured with all the yummy elements you would expect. No-one to date has noticed the difference!

Calories: 164
Protein: 19.8g
Carbohydrate: 9.1g
Fat: 5.5g

SERVES 4
WLS portion: ½

Metric / *US*
1 cauliflower, cut into florets
low-fat cooking spray
2 eggs, beaten
salt and freshly ground black pepper
2 cloves garlic, finely chopped
1 small piece fresh ginger root, cut into small strips
1 small red chilli, finely chopped or 1 tsp Lazy Chilli
1 onion, finely chopped
100g / 4oz ham, cooked pork or bacon, cut into strips
100g / ⅔ cup peeled prawns / *shelled shrimp*
2 tbsp light soy sauce
4 spring onions / *scallions*, sliced
100g / 4oz bean sprouts

1. Place the cauliflower in a microwave-proof dish and microwave on FULL POWER for about 4-5 minutes, depending upon wattage. Do not add any water. Place in a food processor and process until it resembles rice.
2. Spritz a large pan with low-fat cooking spray. Season the eggs and cook for about 1 minute until lightly scrambled. Remove, chop and set aside.
3. Spritz the pan again, add the garlic, ginger, chilli and onion and cook for 1-2 minutes. Add the ham, pork or bacon and cook until golden.
4. Add the prawns and cauliflower and toss well to mix.
5. Add the egg with the soy sauce, most of the spring onions / *scallions* and bean sprouts. Stir-fry until well heated through, about 2-3 minutes. Sprinkle with the remaining spring onions / *scallions* to serve.

Low-fat sausage and Pink Lady casserole

There is little better suited to make a speedy casserole than a pack of low-fat, high-meat content sausages mixed with crisp, sweet apples to make a moreish mouthful. It is all the more superior for adding a spoonful of cranberry sauce. I make my own (using sweetener) but you can use commercial varieties if you are confident in being able to tolerate just a small amount of sugar, otherwise leave out, the apples add enough sweetness of their own.

Calories: 305
Protein: 18.1g
Carbohydrate: 33.6g
Fat: 10.9g

SERVES 2
WLS portion: ½

Metric / *US*
4 extra-lean, low-fat sausages
low-fat cooking spray
1 red onion, finely sliced
1 large sprig rosemary, leaves only
2 Pink Lady apples, cut into wedges
1 tbsp cranberry sauce (optional)
1 tbsp wholegrain mustard
200ml / *generous 1 cup* vegetable stock / *bouillon*
salt and freshly ground black pepper

1. Grill / *broil* the sausages according to the packet instructions then thickly slice.
2. Meanwhile, generously spritz a pan with low-fat cooking spray. Heat then add the onion and cook until soft and golden, about 8-10 minutes.
3. Add the rosemary and apples and cook for 3-4 minutes until the apples start to soften. Add the cranberry sauce if used, mustard, sliced sausages, stock / *bouillon* and salt and pepper to taste. Simmer uncovered for about 10 minutes. Thicken with a little cornflour / *cornstarch* mixed with water if liked.
4. Serve hot, it's delicious with boiled new potatoes.

Comforting cassoulet

This substantial dish takes just minutes to prepare, is full of flavour and cooks quickly too. You can vary the recipe by using different canned beans such as red kidney or a mixed can and use a different kind of sausage. It's also a great freezer standby for those occasions when you don't want to cook from scratch. This is a hearty dish that doesn't need much more than a light salad accompaniment.

Calories: 381
Protein: 42.9g
Carbohydrate: 36.4g
Fat: 7.9g

SERVES 4
WLS portion: ½

Metric / US
low-fat cooking spray
4 reduced-fat pork chipolata sausages (about 225g / 8oz)
1 large onion, sliced
400g / 14oz skinless and boneless chicken breasts,
    cut into bite-sized pieces
1 tsp smoked paprika / *smoked paprika pepper*
2 x 400g / 14oz cans chopped tomatoes
410g / 14oz can cannellini beans, drained and rinsed
420g / 15oz can butter beans, drained and rinsed
15g / ½oz fresh oregano, chopped
salt and freshly ground black pepper

1. Generously spritz a large, deep, non-stick sauté or frying pan with the low-fat cooking spray. Heat, add the sausages and cook for 3-4 minutes until lightly browned on all sides.
2. Remove the sausages from the pan and set aside. Spritz the pan again, add the onion, chicken and paprika / *smoked paprika pepper* and cook for 4-5 minutes until the chicken is browned and the onion has softened.
3. Return the sausages to the pan with the tomatoes, cannellini beans, butter beans, half of the oregano and salt and pepper to taste, mixing well. Bring to the boil, cover and simmer for 30-40 minutes, stirring occasionally, until the chicken is tender and cooked and the sauce has thickened. If necessary, remove the lid for the final 5 minutes cooking time to reduce the sauce.
4. Serve hot garnished with the remaining oregano.

Guilt-free comfort food

Sometimes, and regardless of time of year, all you hanker for is a bowl of something warm and comforting to eat. Well here are the recipes to make when that time comes. They are comfort food classics that have been given the bariatric once-over so that they offer nurture with nourishment.

SERVES 4
WLS portion: ½

Calories: 398
Protein: 31.3g
Carbohydrate: 50g
Fat: 9.2g

Turkey cottage pie

Metric / US

Preheat the oven to 200°C / 400°F / gas mark 6. Spritz a pan with low-fat cooking spray. Add 1 chopped onion, leek and carrot and cook for 10 minutes. Remove from the pan and set aside. Spritz the pan again, add 450g / 1lb turkey mince / ground turkey and cook for 5 minutes. Add the vegetable mixture, 1 tbsp Worcestershire sauce, 400g / 14oz can chopped tomatoes, 100g / 4oz frozen peas, 1 tbsp tomato paste, 1 tsp chopped fresh thyme and salt and pepper to taste. Cook for 20 minutes until tender. Spoon into a shallow ovenproof dish. Meanwhile, cook 1kg / 2¼lb potatoes until tender then mash with seasoning to taste. Spoon over the turkey mixture and sprinkle with 25g / ¼ cup grated low-fat cheese. Bake for 30 minutes until golden.

VARIATION

Turkey and bean cottage pie: Prepare as above but add a 200g / 7oz can baked beans or curried beans to the cooked turkey mixture before topping with the mashed potato.

Lamb's liver with caramelised onions

Metric / *US*

Spritz a large, heavy-based frying pan with low-fat cooking spray. Heat gently, then add 2 thinly-sliced onions and cook over a low heat for 10-15 minutes, until the onion is golden. Push the onions to one side of the pan and add 300g / *11oz* sliced lamb's liver and fry gently on each side for 1-2 minutes until lightly browned. Add 90ml / *½ cup* water and 3 tbsp balsamic glaze and stir until the liver and onions are coated in a glossy juice. Serve hot with a herby mash if liked.

SERVES 2
WLS portion: ½

Calories: 273
Protein: 31.6g
Carbohydrate: 14.4g
Fat: 9.7g

Easy fisherman's pie

Metric / *US*

Preheat the oven to 180°C / 350°F / gas mark 4. Cut 450g / *1lb* assorted fresh and smoked fish into bite-sized pieces. Place in a heatproof baking dish with 100g / *⅔ cup* peeled prawns / *shelled shrimp*. Dot with a 150g / *5oz* tube soft cheese or 150g / *5oz* extra-light soft cheese as liked. Sprinkle with the juice of 1 lemon, 3 tbsp snipped chives and salt and pepper to taste. Meanwhile, cook 1.4kg / *3lb* peeled and chopped potatoes until tender then mash with 125g / *4oz* fat-free Greek yogurt and seasoning to taste. Spread over the fish mixture and bake for 45-50 minutes until cooked and golden.

SERVES 6
WLS portion: ½

Calories: 350
Protein: 25.9g
Carbohydrate: 44.1g
Fat: 8.1g

Most tender roast chicken with vegetable gratin

Roast chicken can be most troublesome if it is cooked too dry and tough. This is my perfected method to cook, using a roasting bag, that gives mouth-watering, tender results. Serve with a cheesy vegetable gratin.

Calories: 300
Protein: 40.1g
Carbohydrate: 20.2g
Fat: 6.7g

SERVES 4
WLS portion: ½

Metric / *US*
1.75kg / *4lb* chicken
2 tbsp low-fat spread
1 tbsp chopped fresh thyme
1 clove garlic, crushed
salt and freshly ground black pepper
2 quarters unwaxed lemon

1. Preheat the oven to 220°C / 425°F / gas mark 7. Mix the spread with the thyme, garlic and seasoning. Slide half under the loosened breast skin of the chicken. Smear the rest over the breast and place inside a roasting bag with the lemon. Roast, breast-side down for 20 minutes. Reduce temperature to 180°C / 350°F / gas mark 4 and cook for 30 minutes.
2. Turn breast side up, slit the bag (so the chicken browns). Roast for 40 minutes until cooked. Allow to stand for 10 minutes before carving and serving with the gratin.

Vegetable gratin

Cook 2 sliced onions, 2 cloves garlic and 3 sliced courgettes / *zucchini* in low-fat cooking spray for 5 minutes. Mix with 300g / *10oz* sliced tomatoes and 1 tsp chopped tarragon. Top with 50g / *1 cup* breadcrumbs mixed with 100g / *1 cup* grated low-fat cheese. Cover and bake with the chicken for 30 minutes. Uncover and bake for 10 minutes to brown.

Bariatric pizza

I still think my pizza recipe using a low-carb tortilla (in 'Return to Slender 1') is quite sensational...but I do know that quite a few bariatrics have a problem with bread or wheat-based products, so this is an alternative that should suit all.

It's easy, believe me, it takes less than a minute to grate a courgette / *zucchini* and mix with some grated cheese and beaten egg, then cook to make a digestible base. The topping here is just an idea, look in your refrigerator and there is probably everything you need.

Oh, and by the way, it's great cold too!

Calories: 220
Protein: 24.3g
Carbohydrate: 8.6g
Fat: 10.1g

SERVES 2
WLS portion: ½

Metric / *US*

1 large courgette / *zucchini* grated
1 egg, beaten
125g / 4oz light or half-fat mozzarella cheese, grated
salt and freshly ground black pepper
Topping:
2-3 / 3-4 tbsp tomato passata or paste
4 slices wafer-thin cooked ham, chopped or 2-3 thin
    slices of Prosciutto
50g / ¼ cup sliced light or half-fat mozzarella cheese
6 cherry tomatoes, halved
1 small handful of rocket leaves

1. Preheat the oven to 190°C / 375°F / gas mark 5. Line a baking tray with silicone paper or easy glide.
2. Mix the grated courgette / *zucchini* with the egg, grated mozzarella and salt and pepper to taste. Pour onto the tray and shape into a round pizza base. Bake in the oven for 20-25 minutes or until light golden in colour. Remove from the oven and leaving on the paper or easy glide, lift off the tray and allow to cool.
3. Increase the oven temperature to 220°C / 425°F / gas mark 7. Spread the tomato passata or paste over the prepared base, then top with the ham, sliced cheese and cherry tomatoes. Return to the tray and oven, and bake for about 10 minutes or until the cheese is bubbling.
4. Sprinkle over the rocket and cut into wedges to serve.

Veggie fest

I am not a vegetarian but I often have a meatless meal, sometimes by choice and often by chance. Depending upon what is at the market, in the refrigerator, freezer or store cupboard I often whip up a dish and find that the components sing loud and clear without the fish, fowl or meat addition. These are some that have become family favourites when we have a veggie fest.

SERVES 4
WLS portion: ½

Calories: 143
Protein: 11.8g
Carbohydrate: 13.6g
Fat: 4.8g

Cheesy baked marrow

Metric / US

Preheat the oven to 200°C / 400°F / gas mark 6. Spritz a large baking dish with low-fat oil spray then add 8 thick slices of deseeded marrow / zucchini squash. Generously spritz a large pan with low-fat cooking spray, heat, then add 1 chopped onion, 2 chopped sticks / stalks celery and 1 chopped red or yellow pepper / capsicum and cook for 3-4 minutes. Remove from the heat and stir in 50g / 2oz frozen sweetcorn, 50g / 2oz frozen peas, 75g / ¾ cup grated half-fat hard cheese, 40g / ¾ cup fresh wholemeal breadcumbs, 1 tbsp snipped chives and salt and freshly ground black pepper to taste. Use to stuff the marrow / zucchini squash. Mix a further 25g / ¼ cup grated half-fat hard cheese with 15g / ¼ cup fresh wholemeal breadcumbs and sprinkle over the top. Cover with foil and bake for 25 minutes, removing the foil for the last 10 minutes.

Quorn and rice stuffed peppers

Metric / US

Preheat the oven to 200°C / 400°F / gas mark 6. Halve 4 red or yellow peppers / *capsicums*. Spritz with low-fat cooking spray and bake for 10 minutes. Meanwhile, spritz a pan with low-fat cooking spray, add 450g / *1lb* Quorn mince / *ground Quorn*, 1 chopped onion and 1 crushed clove garlic. Cook for 5 minutes. Add a 400g / *14oz* can chopped tomatoes, 2 tbsp tomato paste and 250ml / *generous 1 cup* vegetable stock / *bouillon*. Cook for 10 minutes. Add 200g / *1⅓ cups* cooked rice, a drained 400g / *14oz* can kidney beans and seasoning to taste. Swirl a little light cheese from half a 150g / *5oz* tube inside each pepper / *capsicum* and top with the Quorn. Bake for 10 minutes. Top with the remaining cheese to serve.

SERVES 4
WLS portion: ½

Calories: 370
Protein: 31.5g
Carbohydrate: 43.8g
Fat: 6.4g

Vegetable chilli

Metric / US

Generously spritz a large, non-stick pan with low-fat cooking spray. Heat, then add 1 sliced onion and cook for 5 minutes until softened. Add 2 deseeded red peppers / *capsicums*, chopped into bite-sized chunks and cook for 2 minutes. Add 1 tbsp mild chilli powder and cook for 1 minute. Stir in 1 large chopped carrot, 2 peeled and chopped sweet potatoes, a 400g / *14oz* can chopped tomatoes with garlic and 200ml / *generous 1 cup* vegetable stock / *bouillon* and simmer for 15-20 minutes. Add 1 chopped courgette / *zucchini* and a 400g / *14oz* can kidney beans in chilli sauce and simmer for 5 minutes. Finally add 50g / *2oz* green beans and simmer for 5-10 minutes until tender. Serve hot with rice if liked.

SERVES 6
WLS portion: ½ - ¾

Calories: 150
Protein: 6.9g
Carbohydrate: 27.7g
Fat: 1.7g

Quorn, tomato and yogurt bake

This Greek-inspired bake, layered with minced Quorn / *ground Quorn* and sliced tomatoes, makes a very good family supper dish. If you have the time, make the Quorn filling up to 24 hours ahead to allow the flavours to develop. Cover and leave to cool, then chill until ready to assemble and bake (adding an extra 10 minutes to the cooking time). A delicious dish to serve with a crisp salad.

Calories: 240
Protein: 26.7g
Carbohydrate: 18.2g
Fat: 5.8g

SERVES 4
WLS portion: ½

Metric / *US*
low-fat cooking spray
450g / *1lb* frozen minced Quorn / *ground Quorn*
2 x 400g / *14oz* cans chopped tomatoes with herbs
½ tsp dried rosemary
salt and freshly ground black pepper
3 large slicing tomatoes, thinly sliced
150g / *5oz* pot fat-free Greek yogurt
1 egg, beaten
25g / *¼ cup* grated Parmesan cheese

1. Preheat the oven to 200°C / 400°F / gas mark 6.
2. Generously spritz a large non-stick pan with low-fat cooking spray. Add the Quorn and cook, stirring occasionally, for 5 minutes.
3. Stir in the canned tomatoes, rosemary and salt and pepper to taste. Simmer for 15-20 minutes until cooked and slightly thickened.
4. In the base of a 23 x 19 x 4 cm / *9 x 7 x 2 inch* lasagne or baking dish, place a layer of sliced tomatoes, then spoon over half of the Quorn mixture. Repeat with more tomato slices and then the remaining Quorn. Finally top with the remaining tomato slices.
5. Mix the yogurt with the egg and a little seasoning to taste and spoon over the top. Sprinkle with the Parmesan and bake for 30-35 minutes, or until the top is starting to brown.

Roasted harissa vegetables with giant couscous

You could use ordinary couscous for this dish but the giant type has a much nuttier, roasted flavour and more satisfying texture. I have used a wholewheat version that is topped with roasted vegetables flavoured with harissa paste. The vegetables could be mixed with cooked chicken, cheese or chick peas for additional protein. This is a versatile dish that can be eaten hot or cold.

Calories: 260
Protein: 10g
Carbohydrate: 51.6g
Fat: 2.3g

SERVES 6
WLS portion: ½

Metric / *US*

1 medium aubergine / *eggplant*, trimmed
2 medium courgettes / *zucchini*, trimmed
1 green pepper / *capsicum*, cored
1 yellow pepper / *capsicum*, cored
1 large sweet potato, peeled
2 red onions, peeled and cut into wedges
1-2 tsp rose harissa paste
salt and freshly ground black pepper
low-fat olive oil cooking spray
450g / *1lb* cherry tomatoes
few sprigs of fresh thyme
300g / *10oz* giant wholewheat couscous
vegetable stock / *bouillon* cube or powder

1. Preheat the oven to 230°C / 450°F / gas mark 8.
2. Cut the aubergine / *eggplant*, courgettes / *zucchini*, peppers / *capsicums* and sweet potato into pieces and mix with the onion, harissa paste and salt and pepper to taste. Place in a large, non-stick baking pan and spritz with the cooking spray. Cook in the oven for 30 minutes.
3. Add the tomatoes and thyme, mixing well. Spritz again with spray and cook for a further 10-15 minutes.
4. Meanwhile, cook the couscous according to the packet instructions with vegetable stock / *bouillon*. Serve warm or cold topped with the hot or cold roasted vegetables.

Salmon tagine

This Moroccan inspired dish of salmon infused with herbs, spices, fruit and nuts is perfect to serve with couscous (flavoured with grated orange zest). Make sure that the tagine simmers gently so that the chunks of fish do not break up.

Calories: 379
Protein: 26.3g
Carbohydrate: 32.7g
Fat: 15.4g

SERVES 4
WLS portion: ½

Metric / *US*
450g / *1lb* salmon fillets, skinned and cut into chunks
juice of 1 orange
low-fat cooking spray
1 large red onion, chopped
1 clove garlic, crushed
2 tsp grated fresh root ginger
½ tsp ground cinnamon
1 tsp ground coriander / *cilantro*
100ml / *generous ½ cup* vegetable stock / *bouillon*
12 pitted ready-to-eat prunes, chopped
6 ready-to-eat apricots, chopped
25g / *¼ cup* chopped pistachio nuts
2 tbsp chopped fresh coriander / *cilantro*
salt and freshly ground black pepper

1. Mix the salmon chunks with the orange juice and set aside.
2. Generously spritz a large pan with low-fat cooking spray, add the onion and cook for about 3 minutes to soften. Add the garlic, ginger, cinnamon and coriander / *cilantro* and cook for 1 minute.
3. Add the salmon and orange juice to the pan with the stock / *bouillon*, prunes, apricots and pistachio nuts. Stir in the coriander / *cilantro* with salt and pepper to taste. Cover and simmer gently for 8-10 minutes.
4. Serve hot with freshly-cooked couscous.

Come dine with me

Eating out and entertaining can puzzle and challenge many WLS patients. It needn't be so, check out the tips on pages 7-8 for the former and here is a menu for special dining with others at home for the latter. The secret to making it easy is in the advance preparation...both the soup and pudding can be made well ahead and the sauce for the salmon can be heated at the last minute, leaving you time to enjoy the festivities with friends. The best bit of course is knowing that what you are eating is bariatric-friendly and you can eat as little or as much of it without hurting the host's or hostess' feelings!

Perfect pea and lettuce soup

Metric / US

Warm a large pan, spritz with low-fat sunflower oil spray then add 1 bunch chopped spring onions / *scallions*, 2 diced courgettes / *zucchini* and a crushed clove of garlic. Cook for 3-4 minutes. Add 1 head / *heart* shredded Little Gem lettuce and 900ml / *3¾ cups* vegetable stock / *bouillon*. Bring to the boil then simmer for 2-3 minutes. Add 300g / *10oz* fresh or frozen peas and 1 tsp Splenda granulated sweetener (optional) and cook for 5 minutes. Purée until smooth. Season to taste and reheat until hot. Add a small swirl of low-fat natural yogurt to each portion before serving.

SERVES 4
WLS portion: ½

Calories: 98
Protein: 7.8g
Carbohydrate: 12.5g
Fat: 2g

Grilled salmon with a lemon, parsley and caper sauce

Metric / US

Preheat the grill / *broiler*. Arrange 4 x 150g / *5oz* skinless Wild Alaska salmon fillets on a rack and sprinkle with the juice of 2 lemons. Cook for 6-8 minutes. Meanwhile, put 225g / *8oz* low-fat soft cheese in a small non-stick pan and heat gently. Add 6 tbsp skimmed milk, grated zest of 2 lemons, 4 tbsp chopped fresh parsley, 4 tbsp capers and salt and pepper to taste. Heat until well blended. Serve the cooked salmon with the sauce and perhaps some new potatoes and green vegetables in season.

SERVES 4
WLS portion: ½

Calories: 212
Protein: 34.8g
Carbohydrate: 4.8g
Fat: 5.9g

Passion fruit and mango soufflés

Metric / US

Tie a folded strip of baking parchment around the top of 4 small ramekin dishes. Blend 300g / *10oz* mango flesh with 3 tbsp Splenda granulated sweetener until smooth. Put 5 sheets leaf gelatine in enough cold water to cover and soak for 5 minutes. Drain and put in a pan with 2 tbsp water and heat gently to dissolve. Cool slightly then stir into the mango. Whisk 3 egg whites until stiff and 150ml reduced-fat double cream / *⅔ cup reduced-fat heavy cream* until thick. Fold both into the mango then spoon into the ramekins and chill to set. To decorate, heat the flesh of 2 passion fruit with 2 tbsp Splenda granulated sweetener until dissolved. Cool and spoon over the soufflés. Remove the paper 'collars' to serve.

SERVES 4
WLS portion: ½ - ¾

Calories: 181
Protein: 5.8g
Carbohydrate: 14.3g
Fat: 11.5g

Wild Alaska pollock and noodle stir fry

It would be hard to find a speedier to cook and more nourishing dish than this one. A bag of frozen pollock fillets and packet of stir-fried vegetables in the freezer, and a package of dried egg noodles in the store cupboard, means that you can have a meal on the table in minutes. You can, of course, use fresh stir-fry vegetables if you prefer. Remember to stir-fry the frozen fish chunks carefully so that they don't break up too much during cooking.

Calories: 317
Protein: 30.8g
Carbohydrate: 39.4g
Fat: 3.2g

SERVES 4
WLS portion: ½

Metric / US
200g / 7oz dried medium egg noodles
2 tsp vegetable stock / *bouillon* powder or a crumbled stock / *bouillon cube*
low-fat cooking spray
500g / 1lb frozen Wild Alaska pollock, cut into chunks
500g / 1lb fresh or frozen stir-fry vegetables
1 tsp Chinese 5 spice powder
soy sauce, chilli sauce and freshly ground black pepper to season

1. Put the egg noodles in a bowl and cover with boiling water. Add the stock / *bouillon* powder and stir gently to mix. Leave to soak for 6 minutes.
2. Meanwhile, heat a wok or large frying pan and spritz generously with low-fat cooking spray. Add the fish chunks and cook, over a medium heat, for about 5-6 minutes, until cooked. Remove from the pan and set aside.
3. Re-spritz the pan with low-fat cooking spray, add the vegetables and Chinese 5 spice powder and continue to stir-fry for 3-4 minutes or until the vegetables are tender-crisp.
4. Drain the noodles thoroughly then add to the stir-fry mixture and gently mix through with the chunks of fish. Season to taste with soy sauce, chilli sauce and freshly ground black pepper. Serve at once.

Massaman lamb curry

This Thai-style Massaman curry with potatoes, coconut and optional peanuts, is less spicy than the more familiar green or red Thai curries. Serve with a little Thai fragrant rice and chopped coriander / *cilantro* for a bariatric-friendly curry meal with class.

 Purée

Calories (without peanuts): 315
Protein: 35.6g
Carbohydrate: 14.4g
Fat: 12.9g

SERVES 6
WLS portion: ½

Metric / US
low-fat cooking spray
1 large onion, sliced
2 tbsp Massaman Thai curry paste
1kg / 2¼lb lean diced lamb
400ml / 14oz can reduced-fat coconut milk
150ml / ⅔ cup lamb or vegetable stock / *bouillon*
350g / 12oz peeled potatoes, cut into large chunks
50g / ¼ cup roasted peanuts (optional)
chopped fresh coriander / *cilantro* to garnish

1. Generously spritz a large non-stick pan with low-fat cooking spray, heat gently then add the onion and cook for 3-4 minutes until softened.
2. Stir in the curry paste and cook for 1-2 minutes. Add the lamb and cook for a further 5-6 minutes until lightly browned and coated in the curry paste.
3. Add the coconut milk and stock / *bouillon*, mixing well. Cover and simmer gently for 1 hour, stirring occasionally.
4. Add the potatoes and simmer for a further 30 minutes, until both the lamb and potatoes are tender. Stir in the peanuts if used.
5. Serve the curry in bowls, garnished with chopped fresh coriander / *cilantro*.

Don't mind if I do!

Party appetisers...

I love a party as much as anyone but despair sometimes at the appetiser food on offer. Crisps / *chips*, roasted and salted nuts, high-fat dips, deep-fried and batter-coated fish and chicken pieces, garlic bread and pastry-wrapped morsels are often the order of the day. What's for me? I think, as I nibble on the vegetable or herb garnish. Well here are some ideas for party antipasto that are bariatric-friendly. Mix and match!

Consider:

- Protein (a must!)...so add chunks of tuna, cubes of cooked meat and poultry, flaked pieces of smoked fish, cooked prawns / *shrimp*, slices of salami or other cooked and cured meats and Quorn style deli offerings.
- Some dairy...like low or half-fat mozzarella balls, cubes of low-fat cheese, pieces of feta cheese, halved hard-boiled / *hard-cooked* small hen's or quail's eggs and quartered pieces of Babybel Light.
- Vegetables...like chunks of cucumber, small cherry tomatoes, quartered canned artichoke hearts, griddled / *broiled* roasted vegetables and crisp vegetable sticks.
- Some pulses...nothing is more surprising and flavoursome than a drained and rinsed chickpea or giant butterbean in the mix.
- A few roasted nuts, like pine or almond, for a bit of a crunch.

- Some seasoned seeds, like sunflower, pumpkin, sesame, linseed and flax, for yet more crunch with nutrition.
- Olives...green, black / *ripe*, stuffed or exotically-flavoured...your choice!
- A little dressing to moisten the combination. Choose your own low-fat version or just a hummous mixture thinned with a little wine vinegar and smidgen of oil.

Serve a selection in small bowls or glasses with wooden cocktail sticks for the ideal one-person portion.

Snack attack!

Now I don't want to encourage a grazing pattern of eating but do recognise there are some times when you just need a crispy fix. Keep away from the fat-laden, ready-made offerings and try these instead. Experiment with seasonings like Jerk, curry, herb, paprika to ring the changes.

SERVES 2
WLS portion: ½ - 1

Calories (for potatoes): 74
Protein: 1.8g
Carbohydrate: 15.7g
Fat: 0.6g

Microwave vegetable crisps / chips

Metric / US
Very thinly slice a 175g / 6oz baking potato (or similar quantity of thinly-sliced raw parsnip, beetroot or carrot). Generously spritz a large microwave-proof plate with low-fat cooking spray. Spread the potatoes (or other vegetables) in a single layer over the plate and spritz again. Microwave on FULL POWER for 6-10 minutes until golden and crispy (times will depend upon wattage of microwave and dryness of vegetable...check frequently). Sprinkle with seasonings to serve. Note: The plate may discolour with prolonged use so use an old one just for cooking this dish rather than your best china.

SERVES 2
WLS portion: ½

Calories: 82
Protein: 6.7g
Carbohydrate: 9.1g
Fat: 2.1g

Crunchy dippers or sliders

Metric / *US*

Preheat the oven to 200°C / 400°F / gas mark 6. Tear or cut two low-carb tortillas or wraps into triangles. Place in a single layer on a non-stick baking sheet and spritz generously with low-fat cooking spray. Sprinkle with salt and any seasonings and bake for 5-10 minutes until just turning golden and crisp. Serve with dips, spreads, salsas and light pâtés.

VARIATION

Crunchy pitta dippers or sliders:
Prepare as above but open up two small pitta breads so that each becomes two flatbreads rather than pockets and tear or cut into triangles. Choose wholemeal, multi-grain, chilli or garlic-flavoured varieties to ring the changes.

Baked salami poppers

Metric / *US*

Preheat the oven to 180°C / 350°F / gas mark 4. Spread a 70g / 3oz pack thinly-sliced French saucisson sec or salami (about 14 slices) in a single layer on a non-stick baking sheet. Bake for 15-20 minutes until crispy. Season with freshly ground black pepper and drain on absorbent kitchen towel. Allow to cool before serving plain or with dips and salsas if liked.

SERVES 4 (about 3 crisps each)
WLS portion: ½ - 1

Calories: 73
Protein: 3.6g
Carbohydrate: 0.3g
Fat: 6.4g

Trifle two ways

Trifle can be the ultimate tea-time treat and whether you opt for the traditional / retro version with sponge, mixed fruit, jelly, custard and a creamy topping; or a Black Forest more modern one with alternative brownie base and black cherry filling, the spoons will be out for more! The recipes below use canned fruit in juice (not syrup) but you can opt for fresh fruit salad or fresh stoned / *pitted* cherries when in season. You'll need about 350g / *12oz*.

Calories: 260
Protein: 10.5g
Carbohydrate: 33.9g
Fat: 9.4g

VARIATION

Black Forest trifles:
Prepare as shown but use low-fat and low-sugar brownies instead of the sponge (see Chocolate brownies with pears and nuts page 73); drained black cherries in juice instead of the fruit cocktail; low-fat and low-sugar chocolate custard instead of plain; and top with sugar-free chocolate pieces if liked.

SERVES 8
WLS portion: ½ - 1

Metric / *US*

23g / *1oz* sachet raspberry sugar-free jelly / *jello* crystals

8 small portions low-sugar sponge or muffins (see carrot and raisin muffins page 74)

400g / *14oz* can fruit cocktail in juice, drained

450ml / *2 cups* low-fat and low-sugar custard

150ml / *5oz* pot fat-free Greek yogurt

2-3 tbsp Splenda granulated sweetener, to taste

150ml / *⅔ cup* half-fat double / *heavy* cream, whipped

1. Make up the jelly / *jello* according to the packet instructions and allow to cool slightly.

2. Break the sponge or muffins into pieces and place in the base of one large or eight small serving dishes. Top with the fruit. Spoon over the jelly / *jello* and chill to set.

3. To serve, top the jelly / *jello* with the custard. Mix the yogurt with the sweetener then fold into the cream. Spoon or pipe over the prepared trifle bases to serve.

Deliciously simple puddings

In the first year after my WLS I didn't have a pudding...unless you count some protein ice cream; some yogurt and fruit; or custard, both set and runny as a dessert (or for the main course!). I can now manage a little more and sometimes enjoy just a small portion of something to round off a meal...so here are some to try...for early days there is an apple purée and yogurt layered concoction; for a little later on some special fruit-laden jellies; and for further down the line a chilled cheesecake that really hits the spot with just a couple of mouthfuls.

SERVES 8
WLS portion: ½

Calories: 230
Protein: 9.7g
Carbohydrate: 23.5g
Fat: 10.9g

Strawberry cheesecake

Metric / *US*

Spritz a 20 cm / *8 inch* springform cake tin / *pan* with low-fat cooking spray and line the base with cooking parchment. Mix 200g / *3 cups* crushed digestive biscuits / *graham cracker crumbs* with 25g / *⅓ cup* desiccated coconut / *shredded coconut* and 75g / *6 tbsp* melted low-fat spread. Press onto the base of the tin and chill to set. Meanwhile, place 3 gelatine leaves in a bowl with cold water to soften for 5 minutes. Squeeze the water from the gelatine, then heat gently in a small pan to dissolve. Beat 300g / *10oz* fat-free Greek yogurt with ½ tsp rosewater, 250g / *8oz* ricotta and 3 tbsp Splenda granulated sweetener. Add the gelatine, mixing well then spoon over the biscuit base. Chill until set. To serve, purée 200g / *7oz* strawberries with 2 tsp Splenda granulated sweetener then sieve. Arrange a further 200g / *7oz* sliced strawberries on top of the cheesecake. Serve in slices drizzled with the strawberry purée.

'Early days' apple and yogurt layer

Metric / US

Peel, core and slice 450g / 1lb apples (use baking or dessert or a mix of both). Place in a pan with 3 tbsp water and Splenda granulated sweetener to taste. Bring to the boil, cover and simmer very gently until very soft, about 20-30 minutes. Mash to a chunky sauce or purée until smooth. Allow to cool, then layer in small glass dishes with 150g / 5oz fat-free Greek yogurt and 4 crushed reduced-fat digestive biscuits / *graham crackers*. Sprinkle the tops with a little grated no-added-sugar chocolate if liked.

SERVES 4
WLS portion: ½

Calories: 170
Protein: 5g
Carbohydrate: 30.6g
Fat: 3.5g

Blueberry apple jellies

Metric / US

Place 5 sheets gelatine in a flat dish and sprinkle over 3 tbsp cold water. Leave to soak for 3 minutes until soft. Squeeze the water out of the gelatine and place in a small pan and heat gently until melted. Add 300ml / 1¼ cups blueberry juice drink and 300ml / 1¼ cups no-added sugar sparkling apple juice and mix well. Divide 100g / 4oz blueberries between 4 glasses and pour over the jelly mix. Chill to set, about 2-3 hours.

SERVES 4
WLS portion: ½ - 1

Calories: 97
Protein: 3.4g
Carbohydrate: 19.9g
Fat: 0.2g

Pear and ginger cake

I just love this cake…it's excellent warm with low-fat or fat-free Greek yogurt; cold with low-fat and low-sugar ice cream or custard; or just plain. The apple and cinnamon variation is also a stunner!

Calories: 136
Protein: 4.6g
Carbohydrate: 16.3g
Fat: 6g

VARIATION

Apple and cinnamon cake: Prepare as shown but use a mixture of baking and dessert apples instead of pears and ground cinnamon instead of ground ginger.

SERVES 8
WLS portion: ½

Metric / US
100g plain flour / 1 cup all-purpose flour
1 heaped tbsp Splenda granulated sweetener
2 tsp ground ginger
3 tsp baking powder
3 eggs
3 tbsp skimmed milk
75g / 3oz low-fat spread or light butter, melted
1kg / 2¼lb assorted pears, peeled and cut into thin slices
low-fat cooking spray

1. Preheat the oven to 200°C / 400°F / gas mark 6.
2. Mix the flour with the Splenda, ginger and baking powder. Make a well in the centre and add the eggs and the milk. Whisk and add the melted spread or light butter.
3. Add the pear slices to the batter and fold in gently.
4. Spritz a 23 cm / 9 inch loose-bottomed, non-stick cake tin or pan with low-fat cooking spray and add the prepared pear mixture. Bake in the oven for 30-35 minutes until well-risen, firm and golden.
5. Allow to cool slightly before serving warm or chill to then slice and serve.

Mini rhubarb crumbles

I am often asked to look at old-time family favourite recipes and make them bariatric-friendly. The fruit crumble is one of many requested. The secret I believe is in making the fruit the show piece; reducing the fat and sugar to a minimum; and looking at the ratio of crumble to fruit. This is a deep fruit dish winner.

Calories: 212
Protein: 6.4g
Carbohydrate: 28.6g
Fat: 8.4g

VARIATION

Apple and raisin mini crumbles: Prepare as shown but use about 700g / 1½lb mixed cooking and dessert apples (peeled, cored and sliced) with 25g / 1oz raisins instead of the rhubarb.

SERVES 6
WLS portion: ½

Metric / US
450g / 1lb rhubarb, trimmed and sliced into
   2.5cm / 1 inch pieces
about 6 tbsp Splenda granulated sweetener
Crumble:
75g / 3oz low-fat spread or light butter
100g plain flour / 1 cup all-purpose flour
100g wholemeal flour / 1 cup wholewheat flour
3 tbsp Splenda granulated sweetener
25g / ¼ cup flaked almonds

1. Preheat the oven to 180°C / 350°F / gas mark 4.
2. In a bowl, mix the rhubarb with 4 tbsp cold water and the sweetener. Divide evenly between 6 ramekin or small baking dishes.
3. To make the crumble topping, rub the low-fat spread into the flours until the mixture is the texture of fine breadcrumbs. Stir in the sweetener with the almonds. Sprinkle over the rhubarb but don't pat down too much.
4. Bake for 25-30 minutes until the crumble is golden and the rhubarb is bubbling through at the edges. Serve hot with low-fat and low-sugar custard, low-fat ice cream or yogurt.

Plum and almond traybake

This plum traybake is delicious warm as a pudding or cold as a tea-time treat. Serve with a little low-fat and low-sugar ice-cream or custard or fat-free thick Greek yogurt if liked.

Calories: 271
Protein: 7.6g
Carbohydrate: 25.6g
Fat: 15.4g

MAKES 12 SQUARES
WLS portion: ½ - 1 square

Metric / US

low-fat cooking spray
225g self-raising flour / 2¼ cups all-purpose flour sifted
    with 2¼ tsp baking powder
2 tsp baking powder
12 tbsp Splenda granulated sweetener
5 tbsp dry skimmed milk powder
3 tbsp ground rice
3 large eggs, beaten
150ml / ⅔ cup vegetable oil
5 tbsp skimmed milk
9 tbsp water
2 tsp vanilla extract
¼ tsp salt
6 large plums, halved and stoned
25g / ¼ cup flaked almonds
icing sugar / confectioners' sugar to dust (optional)

1. Preheat the oven to 180°C / 350°F / gas mark 4. Generously spritz a large baking tin, about 30 x 20 cm / 12 x 8 inches and about 5 cm / 2 inches deep, with low-fat cooking spray or line with baking parchment.
2. Sift the flour and baking powder into a bowl and stir in the Splenda, skimmed milk powder and ground rice. Add the eggs, oil, skimmed milk, water, vanilla and salt. Mix well with a wooden spoon or beat with a whisk until blended. Spoon into the prepared tin.
3. Press the plums into the top, cut sides up. Scatter with the almonds.
4. Bake for 25-30 minutes or until a skewer inserted into the cake mixture comes out clean. Allow to cool slightly before serving, dusted with icing / confectioners' sugar if liked.

Let them eat cake!

'Return to Slender 1' (my first bariatric cookery book) had nothing in the way of baked teatime treats. I only started to look at them when I wanted to take some samples along to support group meetings and realised that these items travel well and could be made bariatric-friendly. The three recipes below are tried and tested favourites and the muffins make a great breakfast treat on the run!

SERVES 16
WLS portion: ½ - 1

Calories: 120
Protein: 4.1g
Carbohydrate: 12.7g
Fat: 7.1g

Chocolate brownies with pears and nuts

Metric / *US*

Preheat the oven to 150°C / 300°F / gas mark 2. Melt 125g / ½ cup low-fat spread with 75g / ¾ cup unsweetened cocoa powder in a small pan over a low heat until smooth. Transfer to a bowl and stir in 35g / 1½ cups Splenda granulated sweetener and 1 tsp vanilla extract. Whisk in 3 large eggs, one at a time, until thick and smooth. Add 125g self-raising flour / 1¼ cups all-purpose flour sifted with 1¼ tsp baking powder mixed with ½ tsp baking powder. Fold in 2 peeled and chopped ripe pears, 1 tbsp skimmed milk and 50g / ½ cup chopped Brazil nuts. Spoon into a 19 cm / 8 inch square cake tin / pan lightly spritzed with low-fat sunflower oil spray. Bake for 18-20 minutes until just set. Cut into squares for serving. Delicious served with orange-flavoured fat-free yogurt.

SERVES 16
WLS portion: ½ - 1

Calories: 140
Protein: 4g
Carbohydrate: 10.8g
Fat: 9.7g

Banana tealoaf

Metric / *US*

Preheat the oven to 180°C / 350°F / gas mark 4. Spritz a 21 x 11 x 6 cm / *8 x 4 x 2½ inch* loaf tin / *pan* with low-fat sunflower oil spray. Mix 2 large, ripe, mashed bananas with 2 beaten eggs, 1½ tsp vanilla extract and 9 tbsp Splenda granulated sweetener. Mix 115g plain flour / *generous 1 cup all-purpose flour* with 115g / *generous 1 cup* ground almonds, 3¾ tsp baking powder and a pinch of salt. Fold into the banana mixture. Fold in 3 tbsp melted butter and 75g / *¾ cup* chopped walnuts. Spoon into the tin / *pan* and bake for 40-50 minutes or until a skewer inserted into the centre comes out clean. Cool on a wire rack. Slice to serve.

Carrot and raisin muffins

Metric / *US*

Preheat the oven to 200°C / 400°F / gas mark 6. Place 12 muffin cases in a 12 hole muffin tray. Mix 225g wholemeal self-raising flour / *2 cups wholewheat all-purpose flour sifted with 2¼ tsp baking powder* with 1 tsp baking powder, 6 tbsp Splenda granulated sweetener, 25 g / *½ cup* wheat bran and ½ tsp mixed spice. In a separate bowl, mix 2 large beaten eggs with 75g / *3oz* melted low-fat spread and 200ml / *generous 1 cup* skimmed milk. Add to the flour mixture with 175g / *6oz* grated carrots and 75g / *½ cup* raisins and quickly stir to combine but not over mix. Divide between the cases then bake for 18-20 minutes.

SERVES 12
WLS portion: ½ - 1

Calories: 130
Protein: 4.8g
Carbohydrate: 18.6g
Fat: 4.2g

Emergency supplies

I believe things go 'pear-shaped' when you're not prepared. You know the times I mean...when you're on the road and all you see are fast-food signs; when you arrive somewhere late and there is nothing on the menu for you; and when you're dashing between activities or work appointments and there isn't the ideal 'food-to-go'. I've been there and now have an emergency supply box in the boot of my car to cope with all these situations...sometimes it has been a life-saver!

You might want to consider putting in your emergency box or tin a:

- Low-fat and low-sugar cereal bar.
- Small packet of unsalted nuts.
- Small jar of low-fat pâté or paste in a jar with crackers (don't forget a small knife for spreading).
- Low-fat and low-sugar protein drink (ideally ready-to-drink or in a shakeable flask).
- Rich tea biscuit or light digestive / *graham cracker*.
- Small bag of mixed seeds.
- Small packet of olives.
- 'Healthy' low-fat and low GI snack or meal-pot that just needs boiling water to rehydrate.
- Small packet of dried fruit.
- Screw-topped jar or keep-fresh container with a little bariatric-friendly cereal and a couple of long-life mini cartons of milk.
- Small bag of soya nuts.

- Small packet of beef jerky or biltong (but keep an eye on the eat-by date).
- Couple of sugar-free sweets / *candies* or mints.
- Low-fat and reasonably bariatric-friendly snack like oatcakes, rice cakes, mini Ryvitas or Melba toast.

Acknowledgements and links

My name might go on this book but I am more than aware that it wouldn't happen if some very special people didn't make huge contributions to its conception, production and delivery.

Countless WLS patients, surgeons, dieticians, bariatric nurses, charity groups / forums and support group leaders should be amply thanked for their encouragement to produce a second volume to the original 'Return to Slender'. You tell me you eagerly await it! I thank for help with advice in the book Gravitas, Nirvana Spa, Streamline Surgical, St Anthony's Cheam, The British Obesity Surgery Patient Association (BOSPA), The Hospital Group, The National Obesity Forum and WLS Info Org, and the many individuals who have given testimonials.

My website team at **eight&four** (www.eightandfour.com) have supported me so well since the beginning (and are indispensable). We now have ambitious plans to move forward...this second book is just a-start. Thank you Amy, Kate, Anna and Charlie!

My friends across the pond at **www.mybiglife.com** for whom I blog, also keep me up to date and tell me what WLS patients want. Thanks to editor Karen Eisenbraun.

Special credit should also be given to Sarah Cooper of **The Clever Consultancy** (www.thecleverconsultancy.com) for her amazing help with my newsletter. Sarah is my IT / marketing supporter and without her **Bariatric Cookery** would be a very diluted version of what you see today. Along with partner Craig, we have so many new ideas for 2012.

Many PR agencies and their clients have helped me with images and recipes to try (and adapt), their help is invaluable. Check out their credits.

My book designers at **RumseyShort** (www.rumseyshort.co.uk) are nothing short of the best and, with our chosen printer, Aaron Printing Ltd, prove a formidable team. Andrea Rumsey (and it's a close run race), only comes second to my husband, when thinking of accolades. I wouldn't want to work with anyone else and

doubtless ever will...her work, inspiration and attention to detail I don't think can be matched. With Rob Short we're a life-long team!

But, my husband Peter, who took many of the photographs for this book and the website, has to get 1st prize for patience, perfection and persistence, we are a good bariatric partnership!

Recipe and image credits

Bariatric Cookery (UK) Ltd
www.bariatriccookery.com (pages 15, 22, 27, 34, 44, 50, 60, 61, 62, 64, 66, 68, 74, 75)

British Cheese Board
www.britishcheese.com (pages 28, 41, 45)

British Lion Eggs
www.britegg.co.uk (page 20)

British Peas and Beans
www.tastesofsummer.co.uk (page 20)

Frylight
www.frylight.co.uk (pages 27, 30, 31, 53)

British Turkey
www.britishturkey.co.uk (page 39)

Love Beetroot
www.lovebeetroot.co.uk (pages 23, 24)

Love Radish
www.loveradish.co.uk (page 24)

Ocean Spray
www.oceanspray.co.uk (page 66)

Parma Ham Consortium
www.proscuittodiparma.com (pages 19, 26, 59)

Pink Lady
www.pinkladyapples.co.uk (page 35, 36)

Primula
www.primula.co.uk (pages 40, 46)

Splenda
www.splenda.co.uk (pages 54, 65)

The Alaska Seafood Marketing Institute
www.alaskaseafood.org (pages 32, 52, 54, 56)

Waitrose, where 6,000 recipes can be seen at
www.waitrose.com (pages 3, 16, 18, 23, 32, 38, 40, 42, 46, 48, 58, 70, 72, 73)

bariatriccookery.com

If you are thinking about, have had or are scheduled for bariatric (weight-loss) surgery – Gastric Bypass, Lap Band, Gastric Sleeve or Duodenal Switch, then this is the UK's number one website to support your new eating regime.

Carol Bowen Ball, a gastric bypass patient, and her team, have the food information, recipes and ideas to nourish, feed and inspire you to eat right with every bite.

It's essential that bariatric patients follow strict guidelines and a new regime concerning protein, fat, sugar and overall calories for weight-loss success and maintenance. Patients also need to adhere to the 3 stages of eating from Fluids (straight after surgery); via Soft Foods; to finally Eating for Life. You'll find advice on what to eat through these stages, the recipes to use and ideas for all occasions.

The blog, updated regularly, has seasonal recipes; foodie news (be it product or equipment related); events of interest including details of some support groups; the latest findings and research on obesity and weight-loss surgery; fashion, beauty and exercise tips for those 'on the loser's bench'; discussions on coping mechanisms for before and after surgery; and anything else food, fat or fabulously-related!

You can also register for the **FREE E-NEWSLETTER** for yet more seasonal and topical food features.

Plus there's your chance to leave a comment or two or make a request for recipes and advice. Please join us…

www.bariatriccookery.com